a Taste of the Caribbean

The Complete A to Z book of authentic
and nouvelle Caribbean cuisine.
Includes Bartending in the Islands

by Angela Spenceley

Design/Layout by Dean Clark

Caribbean Press
Box 79710
Carolina, PR 00984-9710
writer@islands.vi

Printed in India

Dedicated to the beauty
and generous people
of the Caribbean

Acknowledgements

My best friend Harriet and my daughter Roxanne share my first thanks equally. Your words of confidence and encouragement over the years, Harriet, gave me the self-belief to continue despite many obstacles. Roxanne, you also believed in me, and your enthusiasm was a sheer delight. To my ex-husbands' wonderful grandmother, Anna, who ignited the spark for my interest in Caribbean cuisine, thank you for gracing my life. Esther, who worked so diligently for Anna, much appreciation for your generous knowledge. Colby, sweetie, you are the most wonderful and funniest son in the world. I can't tell you how many times you had Harriet, Roxanne and I in hysterics.

Many gifted chefs contributed their visualization of the new Caribbean cuisine and worked with me. Without your help, I could not have completed this book. To my little sister, Tanya, who managed to get both of us in trouble during each and every one of her visits, thanks. To my dad, thanks for eating all those horrible cakes that an eager little girl made. To Don, Geoff, Buddy and Alice, my second family, you've always been there for me; for once, the words escape me in expressing my gratitude. Recognition to Jon Euwema for patiently explaining *I talking lapias, mon* and his generous usage of island colloquialism. Finally, to my very dedicated assistant Karma, there is no way this book would ever have been completed without you. Thank you for your patience and dream.

Angela Spenceley

Introduction

Expatriate. There you have it. Such a romantic word. Webster's New World College Dictionary defines expatriate *to leave the homeland*. Was I an expatriate, I wondered? Evidently, since I have lived nearly half of my life in the Caribbean.

I grew up as an only child in Massachusetts close to the ocean, hence my love for the sea. After school, I spent a couple of years on the *far away* island of Nantucket, just off the coast of Cape Cod. There my eternal love affair with charmingly out-of-touch islands commenced. Much of this book and Just Add Rum! had been written there while dreamily staring off into the endless ocean. Now, things are getting ahead of me here. By a serial chain of events, my travels happily landed me in America's Paradise or as our new advertising slogan would have it, America's Caribbean—St. Thomas, U.S. Virgin Islands.

I met my girlfriend and roommate in San Juan, Puerto and together we traveled to our much-anticipated destination. From the height of the twin propeller plane, the ocean manifested itself as crystal rock candy. Even from the altitude of the airplane, the turquoise view cut clearly to the bottom and was delicately shaded by coral reefs. Tiny islets, some no larger than rocks dotted Davy Jones locker. Later we would learn that tourists would attempt to bring home this astonishing water that appeared to have been tinted with food coloring.

Instead of Fantasy Island, we found ourselves in this immense antique hangar. At any moment the Flying Tigers would land. You know those old planes with the eyes and teeth painted on them? The heat nearly caused me to faint dead away, *lawdy, lawdy, lawdy.* You'll find the meaning for that expression later in this book. At any rate, the important point here is the fact that our luggage was nowhere to be found. Everyone was quite kind and polite to two such unseasoned girls and patiently tried to explain that it would arrive on the next flight. It was suggested that we continue to our hotel and the luggage would be delivered. There was no way that Lynn and I were leaving that to chance. The thought of not having a full arsenal of makeup and toiletries was beyond belief. Nothing like this had ever happened to us and certainly not in the United States. We were in the United States weren't we? After waiting for three more flights and another two hours, we were ready to begin our adventure.

Our destination was Villa Santana, built by General Santa Anna of Mexico around 1857. With West Indian charm offered in abundance, the villa provided a panoramic view of the town and stunning harbor. Apparently with some other extra's as well. I had lunch with the owner's son recently, and now, after all these years, tells me that the villa is haunted. Thanks, John. Shuttered windows, ancient walls made from ships ballast and mortared with molasses, high, high ceilings and enchanting wicker furniture contributed to the tropical atmosphere. Ceiling fans lazily circulated the air and an occasional breeze would startle a gecko, a.k.a. lizard. Years later, I would find the most darling little eggs, perhaps even smaller than a peanut M & M in my closet. My little boy and I made a nest for these in a coffee cup lined with cotton. *Mee son*, we waited forever for those to hatch. I wouldn't admit it to Colby, but those eggs were dead. Really? About two months later, while cleaning his room, the eggs were hatched and no lizards in sight! I keep expecting those lizards to turn up someday.

St. Thomas lived up to and topped all of our daydreams. Villa Santana presented an appealing vista of red-roofed houses dotting a rolling green hillside. Built by the Danes, these houses surrounded one of the most beautiful natural harbors in the world. We had never seen a cruise ship before except on the television. They were majestic in their immenseness. Charlotte Amalie is one of the most active cruise-ship ports in the world. Tourists from all over come to shop in converted rum warehouses, which offer a profusion of treasures. Liquor, French perfume, exquisite jewelry, and crystal could all be had at unheard of prices. Our maid at Villa Santana wore expensive Opium perfume. Gee, perfume must be really cheap here, I thought, and it was to our delight.

Brilliant Bougainvillea in a host of colors clambered up pastel-hued European villas in winding alleyways. Larger than life ferns, dazzling red hibiscus and iridescent hummingbirds vividly colored the island.

Blue stone ruins of old sugar mills and cookhouses were reminiscent of plantation days. Sugar cane was the crop to cultivate with the ensuing production of rum. First slave labor and then indentured servants mercilessly fueled this economy. St. Thomas, unable to cultivate the sugarcane because of its steep hillsides and perhaps with foresight, abandoned the rum business and became a bustling seaport. This has stood the island in good stead, as cruise ships and the commerce of tourism is our mainstay.

I'm sure my skin became ruined at the beach during my early island days. There was just something so exotic and hypnotizing about coconut trees and warm tranquil water. The sand was not only white; it resembled talcum powder. Gentle trade winds fanned the palms and contributed to that *manana* ideology so prevalent in the islands.

Lynn has long since left St. Thomas and I have often wondered if she regretted that decision. Immunity to the heat prevailed so that anything below 78°F is chilling to me. Like so many others before me, the Caribbean has slowly stole into my soul. This book is a dedication and tribute to the beauty and people of the islands, which have so generously welcomed and accepted me. Thank you.

Culinary World and Caribbean History

S ay, those tomatoes are Italian, aren't they? Chocolate comes from Switzerland, right? What about all those potatoes the Russians use to make vodka with? Russians are to potatoes as hotdogs to football. Right?

I don't think so. You're probably asking what this has to do with the Caribbean cookbook that you just purchased. After all, everyone knows that jerk comes from Jamaica and curry can be found all over the islands. Before we begin our delightful delve into Caribbean cuisine, let's take a little trip.

Imagine for a moment a metropolis of breathtaking carved stone temples, palaces, schools, libraries and gorgeous gardens in full bloom with flowers from all over the world. This beautiful city is the trade center of the world with a grid of sophisticated roads, canals and bridges. Now, picture a vast open market filled to bursting with colorful vendor stalls with separate areas for jewelry, produce, spices, flowers, medicines, meats, clothing and a plethora to appease the most particular connoisseur. Mmm, the most delicious aromas seem to be coming somewhere just ahead of us. Barbequed meat, chicken and fish are on our left, tempting meat and plantain-stuffed corn tortillas just in front of us, spicy fish stews and delicately scented soups being ladled in beautiful earthen bowls by the vendor on the right.

Directly across are the fruit and vegetables vendors. Huge shaded baskets are over flowing with squash, tomatoes, chilies, corn, potatoes, papayas, pineapples, cocoa and an abundance of spices. Men from trade caravans are bartering to bring the abundance of the Americas to all over the world.

The year is 1519 and the city is Tenochtitlan, the Aztec capital of Peru. A municipality such as this would impress us today, think of the Spanish Conquistadors who happened upon it.

The agricultural diversity in Tenochtitlan was the final product of thousands of years, diverse civilizations and two continents. Back then there were two primary centers of agricultural modernism, which consisted of the Andes Mountains of Peru and Ecuador and south-central Mexico and the Yucatan Peninsula.

In ancient Mexico, primitive farming methods such as the hybridization of corn to produce larger crops encouraged population growth. Innovative methods of irrigation allowed crops to flourish on otherwise dry and inhospitable lands. Beans, squash, amaranth a high protein grain, chili peppers high in vitamin A and C along with root tubers and avocados were raised. Even though these diets were primarily vegetarian we should all be advised to look at their nutritional soundness. Even the corn was soaked in lime, which in turn caused it to be high in niacin and calcium.

In the Andes beans, peanuts and all sorts of potatoes had been known to grow nearly six thousand years ago. Farming methods centuries before their time were employed such as the use of guano or bat manure to fertilize and encourage higher yields. Entire hillsides were terraced and intricately irrigated to make use of every square inch of land. To this very day, these same irrigation systems are still in use and functioning admirably.

Anthropologists have found evidence in Peru of another grain called quinoa, many varieties of corn, peanuts, avocados, papaya, pineapple, potatoes, peppers, pumpkins and sorts of beans. Their diet was light in oil with most foods baked, steamed or grilled. Many different methods of food preservation and complex cooking and seasoning came about during this era which still exist today as the Indians traveled north to the Caribbean islands.

In the coming centuries as European nations grew more powerful and sent their ships to find better trade routes, the bounty of the Americas reached far-flung corners of the globe. Europe, Asia and Africa traded culturally— resulting in a swap of foods and cooking methods.

The purpose of Christopher Columbus voyage was to seek, gold, land and other riches. When we accidentally hit upon the Caribbean Islands, we can well imagine that he thought he had found the legendary Shangri-La or fabled Garden of Eden. Lush exotic fauna as never seen before by Europeans, brilliantly colored tropical birds, insects and lizards, steep mountains, waterfalls, endless white sand beaches fringed with gently swaying palms, not to mention an abundance of new fruits and vegetables were presented to Columbus instead of gold. The true riches of the new world were the seeds and cuttings sent back to the Old World. Many of the food staples that European cuisine is based on originated from the Americas via the Caribbean. As the world grew smaller due to cross-oceanic travel in the 16th century, hot chile peppers found their way to the Orient, maize to Africa, tomatoes to Spain and Italy, chocolate to the German and Swiss, peanuts used in curries to India and potatoes to the British Isles and Russia. Mangoes used in delightful chutneys found their way to India from the Caribbean.

The more than 7,000 Caribbean islands form a chain reaching 2,500 miles from the tip of Florida to the north of Venezuela. Cuba is the largest, then Hispaniola, which represents Haiti and the new Dominican Republic, Jamaica then Puerto Rico, all of which are known as the West Indies. Quite a few of these islands are no larger than a rock — some are uninhabited, fabled deserted islands.

Caribbean cuisine is a union of the cooking of all the islands. The unusual and exotic produce of the islands is the basis for the spicy meat, chicken, and fish dishes. Fruits such as mango, banana, coconut, passion fruit, guava, star fruit, and avocado delicately flavor pumpkin, plantain, ackee, yams, and other root vegetables. Fragrant spices perfume the abundance of the land and sea.

Four distinctly different cultures have touched the islands: Amerindian, European, African and Asian. First, the Amerindians, Carib and Arawak Indians came from South America to settle in the Caribbean islands. These farmers grew corn, cassava, beans, sweet potatoes, garlic, tobacco, and all sorts of peppers. Pineapple, guava, papaya, cashews and the occasional fish and wild pigeon supplemented their diet. Their Arawaks were thought to originate the grinding of cassava, draining their poisonous juices to subsequently make four for bread.

The next group, European, comprises four sub-groups with each island(s) dominated by its colorful colonial heritage: the Hispanic influencing Puerto Rico, the Dominican Republic, and Cuba; the French, which includes Haiti, St. Martin, Guadeloupe, St. Barths, and Martinique; the British, includes the British Virgin Islands, Jamaica, Barbados, Grenada; and the Dutch, includes St. Maarten (St. Martin is the French side) Aruba and Curaçao.

When Columbus and his men arrived in the Caribbean, they found the available food of the Amerindians to be rather limited. Flour, oil, vinegar, as well as livestock, pigs and cows, were dispatched from Spain.

With the importation of African slaves, a number of new foods and cooking methods were introduced. The slaves, highly bored with the little bits of meat and fish served to them by the sugar plantation owners, decided to spice things up a bit. They brought with them yams, pigeon peas, beans, okra, ackee, and taro. Rich thick stews were seasoned with scallions, parsley, coriander and thyme.

After slavery was abolished in 1838, all the African slaves left the vast plantations. Freed slaves from other islands and indentured servants from India and China filled the huge deficit in labor. These people also brought their own foods, spices and cooking styles in addition to new utensils. East Indian curries, rice, spices, yogurt, and ghee (clarified butter) were added to the Caribbean menu. Trinidad has an especially high concentration of East Indians and their markets to this day reflect this influence. Vibrant vendor stalls carry everything from curry ingredients to mangoes, eggplants, okra, pumpkins, potatoes, fish, meats, chicken, rice, and legumes. Rice still plays an important part in Caribbean cooking.

Each island in the Caribbean has its unique version of hot and spicy rubs, sauces, and condiments. It has been said that the use of hot peppers is directly related to tropical hot climates where parasites could proliferate. Apparently these creatures do not survive well when drowned in irritating and caustic hot sauce. In addition, the fieriness of the peppers induces perspiration, resulting in cooling — another way to cope with heat.

Some islands are spicier than others. Puerto Rico, the Dominican Republic, and Cuba so not employ the fiery peppers, using much milder cousins instead. Jamaica is reputed for its spicy cuisine, but some of the hottest condiments in the world come from the Virgin Islands, a.k.a. Scotch Bonnet, Congo, or habenero pepper. Having lived in the Caribbean for nearly a decade and a half, I tend to put hot sauce on everything from meat pies and fritters, to spaghetti and pizza.

At some point, there has been an intermingling of foodstuffs, spices and cooking techniques between the islands. All these islands use peppers in varying degrees of fire. Ginger, nutmeg, cloves, allspice, turmeric (one of the principal ingredients of curry, imparting that yellow color) and cinnamon are all grown on the islands and appear frequently on menus.

Modern shipping and refrigeration methods, along with the growing abundance in grocery stores make it easy to obtain the ingredients for Caribbean cuisine. Refer to the glossary and only the limits of your imagination to turn ordinary chicken, fish or ribs into a tropical culinary excursion.

Let's begin our tropical adventure!

Contents

Caribbean Sunrise Specials

Pineapple-Coconut Corn Meal Pancakes
Guadeloupe

We found this unusual and hearty recipe on a cruise taken down island to Guadeloupe and Grenada. Creamy coconut and sweetly tart pineapple combine well with the texture of the cornmeal.

3/4 cup water
1/4 cup cornmeal
1/2 cup cake flour
1/2 cup all-purpose flour
1 teaspoon baking powder
1/2 teaspoon baking soda
1/2 teaspoon salt
1/2 cup butter milk
1 teaspoon vanilla
1/4 cup sweetened cream of coconut
2 tablespoons brown sugar
2 eggs, beaten
3/4 cup fresh or canned pineapple, drained and well chopped
butter
hot maple syrup

In a small saucepan, bring water to boil and add cornmeal, cooking for 4 to 5 minutes.

In a medium glass bowl, sift together the flours, baking soda, baking powder, and salt. Mix buttermilk, vanilla, and Coco Lopez in a separate cup, and gradually stir into flour mixture. Stir in sugar and eggs until batter is smooth. Fold in cornmeal.

Heat griddle or skillet over medium heat, until a drop of water dances across it. Place a small pat of butter on griddle and ladle batter. Drop one to two tablespoonfuls of pineapple onto top of pancake.
Cook until the surface is full of bubbles and flip. Each side should be golden brown. Serve immediately with plenty of melted butter and hot maple syrup.

YIELD: 4 servings

TIP: To make the perfect omelet, never use more than three eggs. More than three eggs are very difficult to manipulate. A heavy cast aluminum or copper pan works the best as heat conducts evenly. In a hot pan, heat the butter making sure it completely coats the surface. Reduce heat slightly, and add eggs, lifting the edges while cooking allowing the uncooked part to run underneath. Spread filling on top, and cover with a close fitting lid for two minutes, enabling the top to cook. This is important these days because of salmonella.

Creole Black Bean and Cheddar Omelet
Nantucket, Massachusetts

I first experienced this spicy omelet on the island of Nantucket, Massachusetts at the Morning Glory Café. Each summer we traveled from one charming island in the Caribbean to another 30 miles off the coast of Cape Cod. This recipe with its Caribbean-inspired ingredients reminded me so much of home, that I have included my version in this cookbook.

Bean filling:
2 teaspoons olive oil
2 tablespoons minced onion
1/2 crushed garlic clove
1/2 teaspoon chili powder
1/2 cup cooked black beans, canned may be substituted

Salsa topping:
2 chipolte chilies
1/2 cup boiling water
2 teaspoons olive oil
2 tablespoons finely-chopped onion
1/2 sweet green bell pepper, seeded and chopped
2 jalapeno peppers
1 medium ripe tomato, chopped and drained or 2 small canned tomatoes
1/4 teaspoon oregano
sour cream

omelet:
butter
2 tablespoons water
1/4 teaspoon salt
3 eggs, slightly beaten
1/2 cup cheddar cheese, grated

To make bean filling: heat oil in a small sauté pan, add onion and garlic cooking until onion is clear. Add chili powder and beans, mashing some of them, cook another 3 to 4 minutes.

To make salsa: soak the chipoltes in the boiling water in a glass bowl for 1/2 hour, removing stems afterwards and mincing. In a non-aluminum saucepan, heat the oil and sauté the onion, peppers, and jalapeno until the onion is not quite clear. In a blender or processor, mix the tomatoes and all other ingredients except sour cream until blended, but lumpy.

Heat frying pan or skillet as directed above in the tip, basting pan with melted butter. Stir in water and salt to eggs and pour into pan, slightly reducing heat. Lift edges of omelet, allowing uncooked part to run underneath. Spoon on bean mixture and cover with lid, allowing cooking for 1 minute. Spread cheddar cheese over top and cover again for 2 minutes. Turn onto a heated plate and fold over.

Spoon salsa, and top with a dollop of sour cream.

Serves: 2 or 1 hungry person

Sweet Potato Mango Donuts

St. Thomas

Nothing-quite tastes like homemade fresh donuts. What gives these donuts their tropical flavor is a combination of sweet potato and mashed mango. In the Caribbean, sweet potatoes grow on a trailing vine, are orange on the outside, and have white to deep orange flesh.

4 tablespoons butter
1/2 cup sugar
2 eggs
1/2 cup buttermilk
3/4 cup cooked and mashed sweet potato
3/4 cup mashed mango, drained
5 cups all-purpose flour
1/2 teaspoon salt
1 teaspoon baking powder
1/2 teaspoon freshly grated ginger
1 teaspoon vanilla
2 pints vegetable oil
granulated sugar

In large heavy bowl, blend butter, sugar, and eggs. Add buttermilk, sweet potato, and mango. Sift in flour, salt, and baking powder. Mix well adding ginger and vanilla.
Start to heat oil in deep pot to avoid hot splatters.

Knead dough well on lightly floured surface. Roll out to approximately 1/2 inch, and cut out rounds with biscuit or donut cutter.

Drop several donuts in hot oil, frying until golden. Drain on plain white paper towels and roll in sugar.

Yield: 2 dozen

Island Speak: Good night
Translation: Hello, good evening

Banana Pancakes with Papaya Butter

Bermuda

Enjoy the flavor of the islands with this treat. I prefer to substitute at least 1/2 cup whole-wheat or multi grain flour for the all-purpose flour in the recipe. The tartness of lime and spice of the ginger enhance the creamy Papaya Butter.

1 1/2 cups all-purpose flour
1 tablespoon baking powder
1/2 teaspoon salt
2 eggs, beaten
3/4 cup water
1 teaspoon vanilla
2 tablespoons melted butter
1 tablespoon honey
butter for cooking pancakes

Papaya Butter;
1/2 cup fresh papaya, peeled, seeded and cubed
1/2 cup butter, softened at room temperature
1/4 cup passion fruit juice concentrate
zest and juice of one lime
1/2 teaspoon fresh grated ginger
4 tablespoons honey
maple syrup
butter

In a large glass bowl, sift together dry ingredients. In a separate container, combine eggs, water, vanilla, butter, and honey. Gradually beat into flour mixture.

Brush a heavy frying pan with butter and heat until a drop of water sizzles. Ladle the batter on and cook each side until golden. Serve with Papaya Butter.

Whirl all ingredients in a food processor or blender until smooth. Cook over a double boiler until mixture thickens. Allow cooling slightly. Serve with warmed maple syrup and butter over pancakes.

Yield: 6 servings

Tip: Poached eggs are a wonderful, low-fat way to cook an egg, if done properly. The white should be cooked all through and encase the yolk, which when cut should be just a bit runny. Using a shallow skillet instead of a deep pot prevents much of the feathering of the white. High heat (212∞F) will set the egg quickly. Adding vinegar to the water lowers the pH and reduces the temperature of the water at which the eggs set, after the initial boiling immersion. Turn off the heat and allow eggs to cook.

Fill an 8 to 10-inch skillet to the top with water, adding 1/2 teaspoon salt and 1 tablespoon vinegar.

Put egg into a small coffee cup and gently slide egg into the water. This can be performed simultaneously with multiple eggs.

Turn off heat and cover. Remove from heat with slotted spoon after 4 minutes, more or less for firmer or runnier eggs.

To prepare ahead of time, poach for no more than 3 minutes. Store eggs in refrigerator for up to 1 day in cold water. Return gently to boiling water, which has been turned off, and heat for 1 minute.

Lobster and Spinach Eggs Benedict
Aruba

Hotels in the Caribbean seem to specialize in Sunday brunches. Brunch usually involves the usual fruits, waffles, and basic eggs, but many heartier entrees are served. Try this island-inspired version of eggs benedict when you have a little time on the weekends. The extra effort will be well worth it.

3 tablespoons mayonnaise
1 6 ounce tin crab meat
1/2 teaspoon hot chili pepper sauce
1 tablespoon minced onion

Hollandaise Sauce:
1 tablespoons water
1 tablespoon fresh lemon juice
3 egg yolks, beaten
1/2 cup butter, softened
1/2 teaspoon fresh lemon zest
2 English muffins, split and toasted

8 fresh tender spinach leaves dipped in boiling salted water for 1 minute, drained
4 poached eggs

In a small bowl combine mayonnaise, crab, onion, and chili pepper sauce. Set aside.

Sauce: in a double boiler, combine water, lemon juice, eggs, and 1 tablespoon of the butter with a dash of salt. Cook stirring rapidly until mixture begins to thicken. Add remaining butter, continuing to stir quickly until mixture has thickened. If something goes wrong, and the sauce is too thick or curdles, beat in 1 to 2 tablespoons hot water. Remove thickened sauce from heat at once and quickly stir in zest.

Arrange the spinach leaves on the English muffins, spooning crab over the spinach. Next, top with the eggs, and spoon over the hollandaise sauce. Serve at once.

Yield: 2 servings

Banana Chutney Biscuits
Turks and Caicos

These quick and easy cardamom-scented biscuits have a sensual filling of banana chutney.

Filling:
3 large, slightly under ripe bananas
1/2 cup tinned, crushed pineapple
1/2 cup fresh and ripe chopped mango
1/2 cup apple-cider vinegar
1/4 cup water
1/2 cup firmly packed brown sugar
1/2 teaspoon salt
1/2 teaspoon fresh grated ginger
1/2 teaspoon cinnamon
1/8 teaspoon cloves

Biscuits:
2 cups all purpose flour
1 teaspoon ground cardamom
2 teaspoons baking powder
1/4 cup sugar
1/2 teaspoon cinnamon
1/8 teaspoon nutmeg
1/2 cup chilled butter, chopped
1 egg, beaten
1/4 cup buttermilk

Pre-heat oven to 425 degrees.

For filling: Bring all ingredients to a boil in a large saucepan until thickened. Lower heat and cook gently for 20 minutes. Cool and set aside

In a large heavy bowl, sift together all dry ingredients. Using two knives or a pastry cutter, cut in butter until mixture is crumbly.

Separately combine eggs and buttermilk, gradually adding to flour. Knead dough slightly and roll out until 1/2 inch or less thick. Cut into 3-inch squares, and spoon a heaping tablespoon of chutney into the middle of each square. Roll up each square. With fingers dipped in water, pinch shut.

Place on non-stick baking sheet and bake until golden, 10 to 12 minutes. Best served while warm.

Yield: 12 biscuits

Island Speak: Oh hek, you must ta bin bawn wid cawl.
 Translation: You were born with supernatural powers to divine or see spirits.

Papaya Pineapple Bran Bread
St. Croix, U.S. Virgin Islands

This sweet and tart bread scores a ten on the nutritional scale and is chock full of exotic fruits and nuts.

3/4 cup all-purpose flour
1/2 cup whole wheat flour
1/2 cup bran flakes
1/2 teaspoon baking soda
1/2 teaspoon salt
1/2 cup sugar
1/2 teaspoon allspice
1/2 cup butter softened
2 eggs, beaten
1 teaspoon vanilla
1/2 cup cubed fresh papaya
1/2 cup fresh or tinned crushed pineapple
1/2 cup chopped walnuts
1/2 cup chopped pistachios

Preheat oven to 350 degrees. Grease thoroughly one loaf pan.

Sift together in large bowl all dry ingredients, except nuts.

In a separate bowl, combine wet ingredients except fruit, beating until light and fluffy.

Gradually beat in flour mixture; fold in fruit and nuts. Pour batter into pan, baking approximately 50 minutes, until a toothpick comes out clean.

Allow bread to cool for 10 minutes and then turn out onto a wire rack to cool.

Yield: 1 loaf

Ginger Salmon Omelet

St. Martin, French West Indies

Certainly a hearty enough breakfast for the most rugged sailor on cold blustery mornings.

1 tablespoon olive oil
1 tablespoon minced onion
1 tablespoon chopped sweet bell pepper, red or green
1 teaspoon freshly grated ginger
1/4 teaspoon crushed garlic
4 ounces fresh, cooked or tinned salmon
3 eggs, gently beaten
1 tablespoon water
dash of salt
butter
1/4 cup grated Monterey Jack cheese

In a small sauté pan, cook the onion, pepper, ginger, and garlic in the olive oil until the onion is clear. Flake the salmon into the pan, cooking for 2 more minutes.

Cook the omelet as instructed previously with the Creole Black Bean and Cheddar Omelet. Sprinkle on the cheese and spoon on the salmon filling. Cover and cook 1 minute.

Turn onto warm plate, folding over once. Serve immediately.

Yield: 1 omelet

Kiwi Lime Crepes with Orange Butter
Tortola, British Virgin Islands

These crepes are fabulous—they were served to us while on a sailing charter in the British Virgin Islands.

Crepe:
1 cup all-purpose flour
2 eggs, beaten
1 tablespoon melted butter
1 1/2 cups milk
1/2 teaspoon vanilla
1/8 teaspoon cardamom

filling:
2 kiwis, peeled and chopped
juice and zest of one lime
1/2 cup butter
2 tablespoons orange juice concentrate
1/2 cup orange liqueur
1/2 cup sugar
butter

Tip: How to cook crepes: Combine all crepe ingredients in a heavy bowl and beat with a portable beater for 3 minutes. Lightly butter a small skillet and heat. Remove from heat and spoon in two tablespoons of the batter, tilting in all directions to have batter coat skillet. Return to heat, and cook only on one side. Flip crepe onto a plate lined with wax paper, making sure to separate all crepes with the paper. They may also be frozen this way.

To make filling:
Combine all ingredients in a small sauté pan; cooking over low heat until bubbly and thickened.

Spoon one heaping tablespoon of the filling onto the center of each crepe, fold in half and folding in half again to make a small triangle. Put all crepes into the sauté pan, spooning the remaining kiwi lime sauce over the top of the crepe. Simmer for 3 more minutes, remove from pan, and serve while warm. Spoon remaining filling over crepes.

Yield: 6 servings

Did you know? Kiwi fruit is native to China? It traveled to New Zealand in the very early 20th century, that country greatly improved the quality of the fruit and had a virtual monopoly on the production of the fruit. Named "kiwi" in 1953 after a flightless bird a.k.a. apteryx (sounds like a dinosaur, doesn't it?) because of its furry brown skin. Kiwi grows on a vine. The fruit tastes like a cross between strawberry and banana. Excellent source of vitamin C, containing twice as much as oranges and lemons, and potassium.

Purchasing: Purchase kiwis that are slightly firm, yielding gently to finger pressure. If too soft, they will be mealy and tasteless. Ripen at room temperature. Store ripe fruit in refrigerator for several days. Unripe fruit will keep refrigerated for two weeks.

Preparation: It is easier to thinly peel this fruit than attempt to rub off the fur with a towel.

Cuban Egg Nests
Cuba

To really wow your guests at brunch, try something they have surely not seen before. Easy and impressive.

2/3 cup grated white aged cheddar
1/4 cup evaporated milk
1 teaspoon crushed garlic
salt and pepper to taste
butter
6 eggs
1 1/2 cups cooked lobster, shredded
1/2 cup frozen peas, thawed
1 1/2 cups julienne potatoes
oil for frying

Preheat oven to 450∞.

In a double boiler, slowly heat evaporated milk and grated cheese. Stir in garlic salt and pepper.

Lightly butter individual custard or baking dishes. Break one egg into each dish. Pour cheese sauce over eggs, around the yolks. Spoon lobster and peas over the sauce, again avoiding the yolk.

While eggs are baking, fry the potatoes until golden and drain on white paper towels. Salt and pepper lightly to taste. Place potatoes over the eggs, allowing only the yolk to peek through.

Excellent with spicy Bloody Marys.

Yield: 6 servings

TIP: To make an elegant cheese sauce in a hurry, use 4 parts sharp grated cheese to one part whole evaporated milk. Skim evaporated milk will not work with this. You can grate in any flavorful as cheese also, such as Gouda, Romano, Muenster, etc. Put in a small saucepan over extremely low heat or use a double boiler. Do not allow to boil as cheese may separate.

Beach Lover's Creamy Poached Eggs

St. John, U.S. Virgin Islands

My sister loves this dish. It has just the right amount of smoothness with a little zing from pimentos and jalapenos.

3/4 cup grated sharp yellow cheddar cheese
3 ounces cream cheese, cut in small pieces
1/3 cup evaporated milk
1 tablespoon white wine
1 teaspoon Tabasco
1 tablespoon chopped pimentos
1 tablespoon chopped jalapeno peppers
2 English muffins, split and toasted
4 eggs

In a small to medium skillet, over low heat, combine cheeses, milk, wine, Tabasco, pimentos, and jalapenos. Do not allow to boil.

Carefully break each egg into the skillet and slide into cheese sauce. Cover and cook for several minutes. With a large serving spoon, scoop ups each egg and place on top of muffin. Spoon remaining cheese sauce over eggs.

Yield: 2 servings

Did you know? Columbus brought the all-important sugarcane to the Caribbean on his second voyage in 1494. Rum and the Caribbean became synonymous. Just about every island in the West Indies manufactures its own unique style of rum. Jamaica's rum is similar to sour mash whiskey. The French West Indies rum tastes like brandy. Further down-island, such as Guadeloupe, rum is made from sugarcane juice, not molasses as in the Virgin Islands.

Purchasing: I don't think there is such a thing as a bad rum. Choose a rum according to the flavor and characteristics that you prefer. There is no need to purchase expensive aged rums, which are consumed like fine brandy, for mixed drinks or pina coladas. Any inexpensive brand will do.

Rum-Soaked French Toast

Bonaire

WARNING! Not to be consumed before work! It's amazing how just a jigger of Caribbean rum can add life to Sunday brunch. Delicious with a heated syrup made from Coco Lopez, maple syrup, fragrant nutmeg, and rum.

Syrup:
1 cup maple syrup
3 tablespoons Coco Lopez
1/2 cup gold rum
1/2 teaspoon nutmeg

3 eggs
1/3 cup milk
1/4 cup rum
1/2 teaspoon vanilla
1/2 teaspoon cinnamon
6 slices slightly stale bread
butter

In a small sauce pan, gently heat the maple syrup, Coco Lopez, rum, and nutmeg.

In a large, shallow bowl, whisk together the eggs, milk, rum, vanilla and cinnamon. Dip both sides of bread into egg mixture, allowing to soak in for 30 seconds.

Heat a lightly buttered skillet until a drop of water dances across the top. Cook each side of bread for 2 to 3 minutes until golden. Serve with plenty of butter and syrup.

Yield: 3 servings

TIP: For the best French Toast, I prefer to buy my bread whole from the bakery. Leave the loaf out overnight without a wrapper to dry out. With a serrated bread knife, cut thick one-inch slices. If you prefer a creamy center, use French bread; otherwise use regular white bread for a drier texture.

Strawberry-Kiwi Stuffed French Toast

St. Vincent

The island of St. Vincent along with 32 other islands, islets and cays make up the Grenadines , under one nation and government.

3 eggs
1/2 cup evaporated milk, whole or skim
1/2 teaspoon vanilla
6 slices stale French bread 1 1/2 inches thick
8 ounce of whipped cream cheese
1/4 cup granulated sugar
2 tablespoons strawberry preserves
juice of one lime
1/3 cup chopped kiwi
1/3 cup fresh chopped strawberries
1/4 cup chopped walnuts
powdered sugar
cinnamon
butter
maple syrup

Whisk eggs, milk, and vanilla in a shallow bowl. Cut a pocket into the side of each piece of bread. Coat and soak each side of the bread for 30 seconds.

Cream together the cream cheese, sugar, and strawberry preserves along with the lime juice. Fold in the chopped kiwi, fresh strawberries, and nuts.

Heat a lightly buttered skillet until a drop of water sizzles. Spoon a full tablespoon or more as can be fitted into the pocket. Cook on each side 3 minutes or so until golden.

Sprinkle with powdered sugar and cinnamon. Serve with butter and maple syrup.

Yield: 3 servings

Huevos Caribbean

Puerto Rico

This popular south-of-the border dish definitely has island over-tones. Not for the faint hearted. Of course, you can adjust the fire to taste.

1 medium onion, minced
1 medium green bell pepper, seeded and chopped
2 large ripe tomatoes, chopped and drained
1 tablespoon olive oil
1 tablespoon tomato paste
1 teaspoon garlic crushed
2 tablespoons stale beer
2 tablespoons mango chutney
1 habanero pepper, seeded and minced
1 teaspoon chili powder
4 six-inch corn tortillas
olive oil
8 poached eggs
1 cup shredded Monterey Jack cheese with jalapeno peppers

In a large skillet, cook the onions, bell peppers, and tomato in 1 tablespoon of olive oil, until the onions are clear. Stir in the tomato paste, garlic, beer, chutney, habanero, and chili powder. Simmer for 5 to 6 minutes.

Brush tortillas with a little olive oil and bake at 350 degrees for 10 minutes.

Place each tortilla on a plate. Spoon tomato mixture on tortilla and top with two eggs. Sprinkle with the shredded cheese and put back in oven just long enough to melt cheese. Serve at once.

Yield: 4 servings

TIP: When handling any fiery chili pepper, wear rubber gloves and keep hands away from eyes and face or a burn can result. Remember to seed the pepper if less heat is desired. Always start with less and add more pepper if needed. For me, peppers that are the hottest are usually best. Even I have had some wicked surprises!

Shrimp Scrambled Egg Casserole

Nassau, Bahamas

This simple casserole can even be made the night before. Perfect for hectic mornings where a satisfying breakfast is needed.

1 small onion, minced
1 clove garlic, crushed
4 tablespoons butter
4 eggs, beaten
1 cup cooked and peeled baby shrimp
2/3 cup evaporated milk
1/2 cup sharp white cheddar, shredded
1/2 cup Monterey Jack, shredded
2/3 cup frozen peas, thawed at room temperature
1/2 cup seasoned breadcrumbs
salt and pepper to taste

In a large heavy and oven-proof skillet with a lid, cook the onion and garlic in one tablespoon of butter until the onion is clear. Add the eggs and remove from heat, allowing egg to set slightly.

Layer shrimp over the eggs.

In a small saucepan over very low flame, heat the milk and sprinkle in cheese. When melted, pour over the shrimp layer. Layer on the peas.

Melt remaining butter in small pan and add the breadcrumbs and toast for a minute. Sprinkle over the top of the casserole. Cover with lid.

Casserole may either be baked now at 350 degrees for 15 minutes or may be stored up to 24 hours in the refrigerator and then heated through.

Yield: 3 to 4 servings

Caribbean Oatmeal with Fruit Salsa

St. Thomas

Even individuals that do not like oatmeal adore this dish. Low in fat and high in nutrition, this quickly-made dish is easy to make for a crowd on a cold weekend morning.

2 tablespoons honey
2 tablespoons limejuice
1/2 cup fresh diced mango
1/4 cup fresh diced pineapple
1 kiwi, peeled and diced
2 cups old-fashioned rolled oats
3 3/4 cups non-fat milk
1/2 teaspoon cinnamon
1 medium banana
2 cups non-fat vanilla yogurt
100% maple syrup

In a small cup stir together the honey and limejuice. Gently toss mango, pineapple, and kiwi coating with the honey dressing.

Cook the oatmeal according to package directions using the non-fat milk instead of water to impart richness, stirring in cinnamon. Slice the banana and cook during the last 5 minutes with the oatmeal.

Divide the oatmeal into 4 bowls. Dollop 1/2 cup of the yogurt into each bowl. Top generously with fruit salsa. Serve with maple syrup at once.

Yield: 4 servings

Island Speak: Las' ratta in de hole leave he tail out. Translation: Get out of a situation before it is too late.

Lox and Bagel with Pineapple Cream Cheese

Martinique

One of my neighbors gave me this recipe, which she brought with her from Martinique. One weekend out of every month she would invite selected friends over for her fabulous brunch. The pineapple cream cheese was one of the top hits.

1/2 cup fresh-diced pineapple
juice of one lime
1/2 teaspoon lime zest
6 ounces cream cheese
8 slices lox
red onion slices
salt and pepper

Fold the pineapple, limejuice, and zest into the cream cheese with a pastry cutter or fork.

Toast the bagels and spread with the cream cheese. Top with a tomato, lox, and onion slices. Salt and pepper to taste.

Yield: 4 servings

Gorgonzola Mango Buns with Cinnamon-Date Sauce

Dominican Republic

The Dominican Republic is home to luxurious Casa de Campo, which covers over 7,000 acres. Literally meaning "House in the Country," this resort has lovely gingerbread fretwork on its Caribbean hued buildings.

1 tablespoon butter
3 large ripe mangos, peeled and sliced
1/2 cup Gorgonzola cheese, crumbled
1 tin store-bought cinnamon buns
1 large ripe mango, peeled and diced
1 tablespoon butter
2 tablespoon Cointreau
1 teaspoon cinnamon
1/3 cup chopped dates
2 tablespoons brown sugar
1/4 cup toasted walnuts
crème fraiche.

Preheat the oven to 350∞. Butter a 9-inch square baking dish. Arrange the 3 mangoes on the baking dish and bake the fruit for 7 to 8 minutes. Pull out from oven, sprinkle with cheese, and set aside.

Place cinnamon buns in another buttered glass baking dish. Bake for 10 minutes according to package directions. Scoop the mangoes and cheese over the top of the buns and return to oven for another 10 minutes.

In a food processor, puree the remaining mango along with the 1 tablespoon butter, Cointreau, cinnamon, dates, and brown sugar. Pour into a small saucepan, cooking until slightly thickened.

Ladle the Cinnamon-Date sauce over the buns, adding a generous dollop of crème fraiche to each recipe and top with toasted walnuts.

Yield: 6 servings.

Pina-Colada Streusel Muffins

Key West

I picked this delightful recipe up in the most picturesque bread and breakfast. Larger than life hibiscus grew over the white picket fence while a humming-bird busied himself close by. Serve with hot strong coffee. The almonds in this recipe are a good source of healthy protein and vitamin E.

butter
2 1/2 cups all-purpose flour
1 cup granulated sugar
1 tablespoon baking powder
1 teaspoon baking powder
1/2 teaspoon salt
1 cup low-fat vanilla yogurt
1/3 cup non-fat cottage cheese
1 teaspoon almond extract
1 1/2 cup fresh diced pineapple
1 tablespoon butter
1 tablespoon canola oil
2 large eggs
1 large egg white

streusel topping:
1/4 cup all-purpose flour
1/2 cup finely crushed almonds
1 tablespoon brown sugar
1 tablespoon butter
1/2 cup freshly grated coconut

Preheat oven to 400° and butter muffin tins.

Sift the 2 1/2 cups flour along with the sugar, baking powder, soda, and salt into a large bowl.
Combine yogurt, cottage cheese, almond extract, butter, oil, eggs, and 1/2 cup of the pineapple in food processor blending until smooth. Add this to the flour, combining gently. Stir in the pineapple chunks—do not over blend.

Spoon batter evenly into muffin tins.

To make streusel topping, combine the remaining ingredients in a small bowl and top the muffins.

Bake for 15 to 20 minutes until a fork comes out clean from the center.

Yield: 12 large muffins

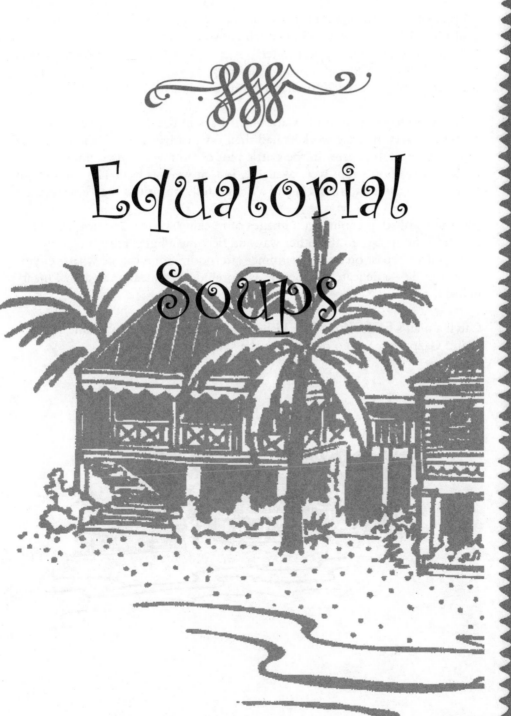

Equatorial Soups

Every island in the Caribbean seems to have its own soup, stew or chowder. In the Bahamas you will find conch chowder, in the Virgin Islands a vast array of pumpkin soups appear, Puerto Rico, Cuba and other Hispanic Islands all have their own version of black bean soup. How about Sopito (fish and coconut soup) from the Netherland Antilles or Jamaican Pepper Pot Soup?

Why is soup so popular in the Caribbean? Back in the days of slaves and indentured servants, the workers had their own early version of the crock-pot. Whatever vegetables grew in their little plot of land were tossed into the pot. If meat or seafood scraps were available, in that went as well. The soup slowly simmered for hours until noon and a delightfully nutritious meal was served.

Just the word soup conjures up images of freezing winters and hot, rib-sticking stews. Soup can go the other way and become a light, refreshing delicately spiced repast on a sultry summer afternoon. Soup can be whatever you want it to be—a delicate consommé as a prelude to a meal or an actual meal in itself.

Catch a man's heart with filling Fisherman's Soup or trim a waistline with icy Island Gazpacho. So, go on and put the soup pot on!

Bahamian Conch Chowder

Bahamas

How many of us as children have ever picked up a beautiful pink conch shell put it to our ears to hear the ocean? I had my first taste of conch chowder actually on the island of St. Thomas. Recipes have a way of traveling in the Caribbean. Gracie's Restaurant served a soup so spicy it brought tears to my eyes. That is also when I fell in love with our little Caribbean hot number—the habanero pepper.

3 tablespoons olive oil
1 large yellow onion, minced
3 cloves garlic, crushed
1 Habanero pepper, seeded and minced
2 quarts water
1 pound conch meat, pounded and sent through a food processor or a meat grinder (coarse)
2 stalks of celery, chopped
2 large carrots, thinly sliced
2 to 3 pounds of firm ripe tomatoes, chopped
1 1/2 pounds potatoes, peeled and diced
4 tablespoons tomato paste
juice and zest of one lime
juice and zest of one lemon
1 tablespoon basalmic vinegar
1 tablespoon fresh thyme, chopped
1 christophene, peeled and diced (you may substitute a cucumber)
2 tablespoons Worcestershire sauce
1/2 teaspoon nutmeg
1/4 teaspoon cinnamon
salt and fresh pepper to taste

In a deep soup pot, bring the water to a boil, add the conch, and simmer for 2 hours. The conch should be tender by then.

In the meantime, use a small skillet, sauté the onions, pepper and garlic in the oil until the onions are soft.

Place all remaining ingredients along with onion mixture in the soup pot with the conch and simmer for another 1/2 hour.

YIELD: 6 SERVINGS

Anna's Curried Pumpkin Soup

St. Thomas, U.S. Virgin Islands

Wonderfully aromatic and filling on a chilly fall day.

2 tablespoons curry powder
2 tablespoons olive oil
1 small habanero pepper, seeded and minced
1 stalk celery, minced
1 large carrot, sliced
2 cloves garlic, crushed
2 pounds yellow or dark yellow meaty squash, peeled, seeded and cut into one inch cubes
2 cups chicken stock
1 cup vegetable stock
1 cup dry white wine
fresh cracked pepper
salt to taste
cinnamon
nutmeg
1 cup cooked, chopped chicken meat
1/2 cup heavy cream

In a small skillet, heat the curry powder for 2 minutes until an aroma is emitted from the spices.

In medium stockpot, sauté vegetables and garlic in the oil until the onions are clear. Add stocks, wine, and spices bringing to a simmer. Cook all vegetables until tender, remove from heat, and cool for 20 minutes.

Puree in blender until smooth. Return to pot and slowly reheat adding the chicken. Remove from heat and stir in the cream. Serve at once with Johnnycakes and dust with cinnamon and nutmeg.

YIELD: 5 TO 6 SERVINGS

Cuban Black Bean Soup

Cuba

For those vegetarians out there, this soup can taste just as good with the bacon omitted.

1 pound dried black beans, soaked overnight and rinsed
2 cups chicken stock
2 cups vegetable stock
3 cups of water
3 tablespoons olive oil
1 large yellow onion, well chopped
4 cloves of garlic, crushed
1 tablespoon fresh coriander, chopped
3 whole cloves
1 teaspoon dried cumin
salt and pepper to taste
1 large carrot, sliced
1 stalk of celery, chopped
1/4 cup dry sherry
1 tablespoon orange juice concentrate
1 tablespoon orange zest
juice of one lime
2 strips bacon, cooked and crumbled
small container of sour cream
1/2 cup yellow onion, minced

In a heavy stockpot, place the beans, stock, and water bringing to a boil. Simmer beans approximately for one hour.

In a small skillet, sauté the large yellow onion, garlic, herbs, and spices in the olive oil until the onion is clear. Add to the pot along with all other ingredients except sour cream and 1/2 cup minced onion. Simmer for 30 minutes.

Garnish with dollop of sour cream and onion.

YIELD: 8 SERVINGS

Did you know? Beans have been in cultivation over 7,000 years starting in Mexico and Peru. With migration, the beans spread over Latin America. Spanish and Portuguese explorers were responsible for having presented beans to Europe, Africa, and Asia. There are over 100 varieties all differing in size, shape, color, taste, and nutrients. Black beans are widely used in Puerto Rican, Mexican, and other Hispanic cooking. Black beans are a good source of folic acid, magnesium, potassium, B vitamins, iron, calcium, phosphorus, zinc and copper. All beans are an incomplete protein, so pair with complimentary proteins such as rice or cheese.

Purchasing: Purchase as dried or canned.

Storing: Dried beans may be stored up to a year in a cool, dry place in a sealed container. Canned beans will last 2 years.

Preparation: Black beans require pre-soaking over night and a cooking time of at least 1-1 1/2 hours.

Antillian Sopito

St. Maarten

Try the light coconut milk that is now available to trim some of the calories off this luscious soup.

1 cup coconut milk
1 cup lump crab meat
1 cup shrimp, shelled and cooked
1 large onion, minced
1 stalk celery, chopped
2 cloves garlic, crushed
2 carrots, thinly sliced
1 scotch bonnet, seeded, and minced
1 bay leaf
2 whole cloves
1/4 teaspoon nutmeg
1/2 teaspoon cumin
5 cups water
1/4 cup dark rum
salt and fresh cracked pepper to taste

Bring all ingredients except the shellfish and coconut milk to a boil in a deep soup pot. Lower heat and simmer for 30 minutes.

Add the fish and coconut milk and gently heat through for 10 minutes.

Serve at once.

YIELD: 6 SERVINGS

Jamaican Pepperpot Soup
Jamaica

There are as many variation of this soup as there are islands in the Caribbean. Here is our somewhat tangy version.

1 1/2 pounds lean stew beef
1/2 pound lean pork, cubed
1/2 pound boneless skinless chicken breasts, cubed
4 cups of water
1 stick cinnamon
1 bay leaf
1 teaspoon chili powder
1/4 teaspoon ground cloves
1 tablespoon fresh chopped thyme
1 tablespoon cider vinegar
1/2 cup cassareep syrup (grated raw cassava placed in cheese cloth, juice squeezed out, boiled until brown)
2 small habanero peppers, seeded and minced
1 large onion, minced
1 clove garlic, crushed
juice and zest of two limes
2 large ripe tomatoes, chopped
salt and fresh cracked pepper to taste

Put all the meats and chicken along with the water, cinnamon stick, and bay leaf in a large soup pot. Bring to a boil, cover, and lower heat. Simmer very slowly for 1 hour.

Add all remaining ingredients except for the tomatoes and simmer for 25 minutes. Add the tomatoes and cook for another 12 minutes. Serve with boiled rice.

YIELD: 8 SERVINGS

Island Speak: Lawdy, lawdy, lawdy, give me faith. Translation: Lord, help me get through this.

Cayman Turtle Soup

Grand Cayman

*Y*ou really don't need to use real turtle for this soup, as it is nearly impossible to obtain. However, there is a fascinating turtle farm on Grand Cayman and they do use the turtles for meat as well.

2 pounds turtle meat or pork loin, cubed
2 tablespoons olive oil
2 quarts of water
1 bay leaf
1/2 teaspoon cloves
1/2 teaspoon cardamom
1/2 teaspoon cinnamon
1/2 teaspoon mace
2 tablespoons butter
1/2 cup flour
1/2 cup sun-dried tomatoes
1/2 cup raisins
1 small yellow onion, minced
2 large potatoes or one breadfruit, cubed
2 large carrots, sliced
4 garlic cloves, crushed
2 tablespoons tomato paste
2 tablespoons cider vinegar
2 tablespoons brown sugar
salt and pepper to taste

Brown the meat in the olive oil on all sides.

Bring water to boil in a heavy stockpot, add meat, bay leaf and spices; simmer for 30 minutes.
Allow cooling slightly, skimming fat from the top. Melt butter in small saucepan, gradually stir in the flour, and add one cup of liquid from the meat. Return this mixture to the soup pot, and bring to a boil.
Add all other ingredients, lower heat and simmer for 35 minutes until vegetables are tender.

Serve with crusty white bread.

YIELD: 6 TO 8 SERVINGS

Fisherman' Soup
Barbados

Angler's Soup or Fisherman's Paradise 1/2

1 teaspoon curry powder
3 tablespoons olive oil
1 large onion, minced
1 green bell pepper, chopped
4 garlic cloves crushed
2 habanero peppers, seeded and minced
1 teaspoon chili powder
2 quarts water
3 medium white potatoes, peeled and diced
1 carrot minced
juice of two lemons
1/2 teaspoon fresh lemon zest
2 tablespoons cider vinegar
5 tablespoons tomato paste
1/2 pound shrimp, cooked and peeled
1/2 pound lump crab meat
1/2 pound firm fleshed white fish, cut up in small pieces
1/2 pound scallops
2 pounds steamed mussels
2 large ripe tomatoes, chopped

Roast the curry powder for 1 minute in a skillet. Heat the oil, adding the onion, garlic, and spices. Cook until the onion is soft and clear.

Bring water to a boil in a deep kettle and add all other remaining ingredients except the mussels, scallops, and tomatoes. Simmer for 25 minutes. Add all other ingredients cooking for another 15 minutes.

YIELD: 6 TO 8 SERVINGS

Gazpacho Carnival

St. Croix

This colorful soup makes a refreshing first course or a light meal in itself.

4 cups, peeled chopped tomatoes
1 small cucumber, peeled and chopped
1 small green pepper, seeded and chopped
1 yellow bell pepper, seeded and chopped
1 red onion, minced
1 jalapeno pepper, seeded and minced
1 clove garlic minced
1 cup vegetable stock, chilled
1 cup vegetable juice cocktail, chilled
3 tablespoons white wine
2 tablespoons fresh basil, chopped
1 tablespoon red hot pepper sauce
1 teaspoon cumin

In a large glass bowl, combine all ingredients, using salt and pepper to taste. Chill overnight. Serve with croutons or garlic bread.

YIELD: 6 TO 8 SERVINGS

Spinach Peanut Soup

St. Kitts

This soup has African origins and found its way down to St. Kitts. Peanuts are also known as groundnuts in the Caribbean.

5 cups chicken stock
1 cup vegetable stock
1 medium onion, minced
1 rib celery, minced
1 small scotch bonnet, seeded, and minced
1 cup natural peanut butter, with the oil drained off
1 tablespoon honey
1/4 teaspoon nutmeg
1/4 teaspoon cinnamon
habanero hot sauce
1 package fresh baby spinach, rinsed, and drained
1/2 cup dry roasted peanuts

Bring the soup stocks to a simmer and add all vegetables except the spinach. Cook until tender, about 20 minutes. Pour into a blender and puree. Stir in peanut butter, honey, nutmeg, cinnamon and season to taste with hot sauce. Blend.

Return to pot and add the spinach, bringing to a simmer. Add the spinach and cook for 12 minutes.

Garnish with the peanuts.

YIELD: 4 TO 6 SERVINGS

Callaloo

St. Lucia

I borrowed this recipe from St. Lucia. Callaloo, spelled many different ways, is the king of all Caribbean soups. Of course, there are many ways to prepare it.

1 pound lump crab meat
1/2 pound shrimp
1/2 pound lobster
6 ounces salt pork
6 cups chicken stock
2 cups water
1/2 pound okra, sliced
1 onion, minced
1 carrot, sliced
1 stalk celery, chopped
3 cloves garlic, crushed
1 to 2 habanero peppers, seeded and minced
juice of one lime
1 tablespoon fresh minced thyme
1 tablespoon fresh minced oregano
1/2 teaspoon cumin
1/2 teaspoon coriander
1/4 teaspoon nutmeg
1/4 teaspoon cinnamon
1/4 teaspoon cardamom
1/2 teaspoon allspice
2 packages fresh baby spinach leaves, washed and drained

Coarsely chop the seafood and pork. Put all ingredients except the spinach in a deep kettle, bring to a boil, and simmer for 1 1/2 hours. Add the spinach and cook for an additional 5 or 6 minutes.

Season to taste with salt and pepper.

YIELD: 6 TO 8 SERVINGS

Haitian Orange Chicken Soup
Haiti

Cointreau is my favorite liqueur for flavoring anything from cakes to chutneys. Try this pleasing version of chicken soup for something different.

5 cups chicken broth
1 cup cooked chicken meat, chopped
1 cup vegetable soup
1 carrot, sliced
1 celery stalk, chopped
1/2 cup orange juice
1 whole orange, peeled and quartered
orange slice
1/2 cup gold rum
1/2 teaspoon cloves
1/4 teaspoon cinnamon
1/4 cup Cointreau
fresh mint leaves
orange slices

In a soup pot, combine all ingredients except orange slices and Cointreau, bringing to a boil. Reduce heat, add orange slices, and simmer for 20 minutes.

Stir in the Cointreau and remove from heat. Remove the orange sections.

Pour into individual soup bowls garnishing with mint leaves and orange slices.

YIELD: 6 SERVINGS

Island Speak: When yo dig a grave, dig two. Translation: Careful what you do to others, it may come back to haunt you.

Tropical Lamb Stew
Martinique

The island of Martinique is often called the Paris of the Caribbean with its French influenced cooking. This fragrant stew is much better on the second day.

2 pounds stew lamb (cubed)
1 large onion, minced
1 bay leaf
1/4 teaspoon cinnamon
1/2 teaspoon cumin
1/4 teaspoon nutmeg
1/4 teaspoon cloves
1/2 teaspoon coriander
1 tablespoon fresh oregano
1 stalk celery, chopped
1 large carrot, peeled and sliced
4 garlic cloves, crushed
1 turnip, peeled and cubed
2 large white potatoes, peeled, and cubed
6 cups vegetable stock
3 tablespoons olive oil
1 cup shredded white cabbage
1 cup sliced mushroom
1 cup sherry
4 tablespoons capers
1 small container sour cream

In a deep kettle, place lamb, onion, herbs and spices, celery, carrot, garlic, turnip, potato and the vegetable stock. Bring to a simmer and cook for 35 minutes.

In a medium skillet heat the oil and sauté the cabbage, and mushrooms. Add to the kettle and simmer for 20 minutes.

Remove from heat and stir in the sherry. Ladle into individual bowls and garnish with capers and a dollop of sour cream.

YIELD: 6 TO 8 SERVINGS

French West Indies Crab Bisque

St. Martin

This is a Caribbean twist on the classic French recipe.

4 shallots, minced
1 stalk celery, chopped finely
4 tablespoons butter
1 pound fresh lump crab meat, shredded
4 tablespoons butter
3 cups fish stock
1/2 cup clam juice
1/4 cup dry sherry
1 cup heavy cream
fresh chives, chopped
paprika

Sauté the shallots and celery in the butter. Put all other ingredients except the cream, fresh chives and paprika in a medium stock pot. Simmer for 20 minutes. Remove from heat and cool for 30 minutes. Reserve about 1/2 cup of the crab meat and puree remainder of crab with other ingredients in the blender.

Return to the stove, gently reheat, and stir in the cream and crab meat chunks..

Garnish with the chives and paprika.

YIELD: 4 TO 6 SERVINGS

Corn and Scallop Chowder
Dominica

This memorable soup came from a quaint little alley restaurant in Dominica. Shrimp or lobster may be successfully substituted.

2 ears of corn in husk
1 small onion, minced
1 tablespoon canola oil
1 tablespoon all-purpose flour
1 cup vegetable broth
1 cup clam juice
1 small carrot, finely diced
2 tablespoons chopped celery
1 pound new potatoes, peeled and diced
dash of Habanero hot sauce to taste
1 pound large scallops
1 tablespoon dry sherry
1/2 cup light cream
1 tablespoon butter, melted
freshly ground pepper

Roast the ears of corn about 20 minutes and cool. Remove the husks and cut off the corn kernels.

Sauté the onion in the canola oil until just clear. Add the flour and cook, stirring constantly until thickened, about 1 minute. Gradually stir in first the vegetable broth, then the clam juice. Add in remaining vegetables and simmer. Stir occasionally and remove from heat when potatoes are tender, no more than 12 minutes. Season to taste with hot sauce.

Add the scallops and cook over low heat for about 10 minutes. Remove from heat and stir in sherry and cream. Pour into individual soup bowls and drizzle lightly with melted butter sprinkling the pepper.

Yield: 4 servings

Island Speak: Yo too biggity. Translation: You think that you're so special, too big for your britches.

Cold Papaya and Anise Soup
Cozumel

This recipe was acquired on a cruise that I took to Cozumel and Jamaica on board ship. It took me nearly a week to coax the chef to part with the recipe—very smooth and light. Use a good, buttery chardonnay in the recipe.

2 pounds of ripe papaya, peeled, cubed and seeded
juice of 1 lime
1/2 teaspoon lime zest
1 tablespoon Sambuca or Anisette liqueur
1 cup sparkling apple juice
1 cup chardonnay

Whirl all ingredients in blender except the apple juice and wine. When smooth, stir in the apple juice.

Chill several hours in the refrigerator. Pour into 4 individual bowls and stir in the wine. Serve at once.

Yield: 4 servings

Island Speak: To blag. Translation: To shoot the breeze, just hang out.

Shellfish Asopao
Puerto Rico

Puerto Rico is famous for its asopaos, a soupy stew. Versions vary from shrimp, crab to chicken. Try to purchase fresh, rather than dried spices.

4 tablespoons olive oil
1 tablespoon annatto oil
4 garlic cloves, crushed
1 small yellow onion, minced
2 tablespoons fresh cilantro, chopped
1 teaspoon oregano
1 teaspoon rock salt
1 1/2 teaspoons coarsely ground pepper
12 medium shrimp, peeled and deveined
1/2 pound lobster meat
1/2 pound crab meat
1 Italian frying pepper, seeded and minced
1 small green bell pepper, seeded and minced
1/4 teaspoon saffron
1/3 cup dry sherry
4 cups chicken broth
2 cups water
2 cups long grain rice
1 large tomato, peeled and chopped
2 red bell peppers, roasted and sliced
2 fresh limes, cut in wedges

For true authentic Puerto Rican flavor use a large mortar and pestle to mash the olive oil, annatto oil, garlic, onion, cilantro, oregano, rock salt and ground pepper into a paste. A food processor may also be used.

In a large soup pot, combine the olive oil garlic mixture along with the shellfish and all other ingredients except for the tomato, dry sherry, water, rice, roasted pepper, and limes. Sauté until shrimp are just pink.

Deglaze with the sherry, adding chicken broth, water, and rice. Cook for 20 minutes until rice is tender. Add tomatoes for last 6 minutes.

Serve in large soup bowls and garnish with roasted peppers and lime wedges.

Yield: 4 to 6 servings

Cooling Tropical Salads

Salads are quick and simple to make and need not be restricted to boring iceberg lettuce, tomatoes, and Italian dressing. High in nutrition, salad is an excellent way to get two or three servings of vegetables and fruits. The following fresh, flavor-packed salads can be served as either a first course or as a meal in itself.

Mango-Spinach Salad with Gorgonzola and Walnuts

Aruba

This is one of my favorite recipes. I always have this salad when I try to diet. It's quite filling, without too many calories, healthy and the Gorgonzola adds a sharp tangy flavor punch.

2 cups fresh baby spinach leaves, carefully rinsed to remove the sand
2 plum tomatoes, quartered
red onion rings
1/3 cucumber, peeled and sliced
2/3-cup fresh-diced mango
1/4 cup Gorgonzola, crumbled
3 tablespoons lightly crushed walnuts
Fresh cracked pepper

BASIL VINAIGRETTE

2 tablespoons olive oil
1/4 cup red wine vinegar
1-tablespoon water
1/2 clove garlic, crushed
1/2 teaspoon fresh zest of lemon
3 tablespoons fresh basil, finely chopped

Arrange the spinach on a plate, and then artfully place the tomato, onion, cucumber, and mango.

To make the dressing in a small cup whisk all vinaigrette ingredients together until well combined.

Pour over the top of the salad. Sprinkle cheese and walnuts evenly over the top. Season with pepper.

Serve at once.

YIELD: 1 SERVING

Seafood Picante Salad

Puerto Rico

Receiving its crunch from cucumbers and celery, the plicate sauce adds Serrano Chile fire.

1 head romaine lettuce, washed and torn
2 large cucumber, peeled and diced
1 celery stalk, chopped
1/4 cup green onion, sliced
3 large ripe tomatoes, chopped
1/4 cup fresh cilantro, chopped finely
1/2 pound, cooked and peeled shrimp
1-cup lump crabmeat or lobster
2/3 cup scallops, cooked and chilled

PICANTE DRESSING

1/2 cup chunky picante sauce, mild
1/2 Serrano pepper, seeded and minced
1 clove garlic crushed
1/3-cup tomato juice
1-tablespoon olive oil
1/2 teaspoon salt

In a large salad bowl, gently toss all salad ingredients together.

In a small pitcher or cruet, stir all dressing ingredients together. Serve with the salad.

YIELD: 6 SERVINGS

Tip: Have ingredients well chilled in advance so salad will be ready to serve at once.

Spicy Cuban Paella Salad

Cuba

This makes a good lunchtime main course. Serve with a chilled Chardonnay.

5 tablespoons olive oil
1/2 teaspoon saffron threads
1 teaspoon cumin
1/2 teaspoon oregano
1 small onion, minced
1 Serrano chili pepper, seeded and minced
3 garlic cloves, crushed
1/2 cup chicken broth
1 boneless skinless chicken breast, baked and cubed
1 large ripe tomato, diced
1/4 cup mussels (out of the shell)
1/4 cup crab meat
1/4 pound peeled shrimp
1/4 pound scallops
1/4 cup pitted black olives, chopped
1 cup cooked basmati rice
6 to 8 hollowed out red bell peppers with tops cut off, roasted in 350° oven for 12 minutes

In a large deep skillet, heat the oil and add the spices, herbs, onion, Serrano pepper, and garlic, sautéing until the onions are clear. Add chicken broth, chicken, tomatoes, and seafood cooking over low heat until heated through.

Remove from heat and allow cooling for 20 minutes. Stir in rice and olives. Refrigerate until well chilled.

Scoop into the hollowed out red peppers.

YIELD: 6 TO 8 servings

Cayman Breadfruit Salad

Grand Cayman

You may substitute white potatoes for the breadfruit in this rich salad.

1/2 cup sour cream
1/4 cup mayonnaise
1 clove garlic, crushed
1 tablespoon brown sugar
2 tablespoons dark rum
2 tablespoons cider vinegar
juice of one lime
1 teaspoon Italian seasoning
1 large yellow onion, minced
1 celery stalk, diced
1 small sweet red pepper, seeded and chopped
2 1/2 cup thawed frozen peas
5 cups cooked breadfruit, chopped

Combine sour cream, mayonnaise, garlic, sugar, rum, vinegar, limejuice, and Italian seasoning in small bowl until smooth.

In large bowl place all vegetables and carefully mix the dressing into this.

Chill for two to three hours.

YIELD: Serves 4 to 6

Tip: Peel the breadfruit, dice and boil just like potato.

Icy Spicy Grenada Salad with Papaya Seed Dressing

Martinique

Papaya seeds add flair and spice to this light salad.

Papaya Seed Dressing:

1/2 cup honey
1/3-cup fresh limejuice
1/3-cup apple cider vinegar
1/2 cup light vegetable oil
1-tablespoon teriyaki sauce
5 tablespoons papaya seeds
1-tablespoon fresh grated ginger
1-teaspoon red hot pepper sauce
1 clove garlic, crushed
6 cups assorted mixed salad greens
1 cooked chicken breast, deboned and cubed
1/2 cup fresh broccoli florets
1 large ripe tomato, chopped
1/4 cup red onion, minced
1 small green bell pepper, seeded and chopped
1/2 cup cucumber, peeled and thinly sliced
1/2 cup raw grated carrot with limejuice sprinkled over it to prevent discoloration
1/2 cup uncooked mushrooms, sliced
1/2 cup finely shredded red cabbage
3 tablespoons, raisins
Alfalfa sprouts

Whirl the ingredients for Papaya Seed dressing in a blender until smooth. Chill.

In a large salad bowl, combine all other ingredients except sprouts and raisins.

Pour dressing over the top of the salad and garnish with raisins and sprouts.

YIELD: Enough for 2

Calypso Salad
Trinidad

For curry lovers only! The fresh flavor of mango and kiwi combines well with the seafood and asparagus.

1/4 cup sour cream
1/4 cup mayonnaise
2 tablespoons mango chutney or pineapple chutney
1-teaspoon fresh, grated ginger
1 tablespoon to taste curry powder
Juice of two limes
2 ripe mangos, peeled and diced
1 cup lobster, cooked and shredded
1 cup shrimp, cooked and peeled
1 cup scallops, cooked
2 tablespoons capers
8 large lettuce leaves, bib, or romaine
4 kiwis, peeled and sliced
1/4 cup grated unsweetened coconut
8 small clusters of red grapes

Combine sour cream, mayonnaise, chutney, ginger, curry, and limejuice in a small bowl.

In a large bowl, toss the mango, seafood, and capers. Add the dressing until well combined.

Arrange each lettuce leaf on a luncheon plate and divide seafood equally onto the lettuce leaves.

Garnish with kiwi, coconut, and grape clusters off to the side of plate.

YIELD: 8 servings

Island Speak: Bragadam, what a mash up. Translation: Darn it, what a mess!

Down Island Spicy Stuffed Eggplant Salad
Cozumel

While on a cruise we came across this delightful restaurant in Cozumel, which served this unusual salad. Marinate this salad overnight to bring out the full flavor of the fresh herbs.

2 eggplants, cut in half lengthwise, and scooped out
2 garlic cloves, crushed
1/4 cup olive oil
3 tomatillos, peeled and chopped
1 large ripe tomato, diced
1 small onion, minced
1 jalapeno pepper, minced
1/2 cup Mozzarella cheese, shredded
1/2 cup Monterey Jack cheese, shredded
1/2 teaspoon each: fresh oregano, thyme, marjoram, basil, and rosemary
1 tablespoon vinegar
1 tablespoon dark rum
2 tablespoons water
Salt and fresh cracked pepper to taste

In a medium skillet, sauté the scooped out eggplant and garlic in two tablespoons of the olive oil for five minutes.

Remove from heat and cool. In a large bowl, combine the eggplant mixture with tomatillos, tomato, onion, jalapeno, cheeses, and fresh herbs.

In a small bowl, combine the vinegar, rum, remaining olive oil, and water. Pour over the salad and toss well.

Refrigerate at least 4 hours. Best on second day.

YIELD: 4 to 6 servings

Virgin Island Sweet Potato Salad
British Virgin Islands

This salad is high in vitamin A and a light meal in itself. Serve with a scoop of sorbet and low-fat cottage cheese.

2 tablespoons orange juice concentrate
Juice and zest of one lime
Juice of one lemon
1 teaspoon fresh grated ginger
2 tablespoons honey
2 tablespoons safflower oil
1/2 teaspoon cayenne pepper
1/4 teaspoon cinnamon
1/4 teaspoon allspice
3 pounds cooked sweet potatoes, peeled and diced
1 ripe mango, peeled and sliced
1-cup fresh cubed pineapple
1/4 cup currants

Whirl in blender the orange juice, lemon and limejuice, zest, ginger, honey, oil, cayenne and spices.

Toss the sweet potato, mango, pineapple, and currants with the dressing. Chill.

YIELD: 4 servings

Parmesan Chicken and Lime Papaya Salad
Cozumel

Use only fresh ripe papaya for this recipe.

6 bib lettuce leaves
1 small ripe papaya, peeled, seeded and diced
2 cooked, boneless chicken breasts, diced
1 cup baby carrots
1 celery stalk, chopped
1 star fruit, sliced cross-wise
1 cup seedless red grapes
1/2 cup mayonnaise
juice of one lime
3 tablespoons champagne vinegar
1 tablespoon Dijon-style mustard
1 tablespoon brown sugar
2 tablespoons water
1/2 cup shredded Parmesan cheese
1/2 cup cashew halves

Arrange three lettuce leaves on each plate.

Gently toss papaya, chicken breast, carrot, celery, grapes, and starfruit. Mix mayonnaise, limejuice, vinegar, mustard, brown sugar and water together, pouring over salad.

Divide the chicken salad between the two plates on top of the lettuce. Garnish with Parmesan and cashews.

YIELD: 2 servings

Island Chicken Salad with Pepper Confetti

St. Thomas

Peppers grow so plentifully in the Caribbean that they find their way into almost every recipe. The same perhaps can be said for mango and pineapple. Careful! Very hot!

1 small pineapple cut in half lengthwise, scooped out and diced, with shells reserved
2 cups cooked, diced chicken light or dark meat
1/4 cup golden raisins
1/2 cup each slivered red pepper, yellow pepper, and green pepper
1 celery stalk, chopped
1 small onion, minced
1/2 cup shredded red cabbage
1-tablespoon fiery horseradish
1/2 cup mayonnaise
1/2 teaspoon cayenne pepper
1-teaspoon red hot pepper sauce
1 tablespoon white wine

In large bowl, combine scooped pineapple, chicken, raisins, peppers, celery, onion, and cabbage.

To make dressing, combine remaining ingredients in another small bowl or container. Fill pineapple halves with chicken mixture and pour dressing over the top.

YIELD: 2 servings

Carrot, Pigeon Pea and Pasta Salad

St. John, U.S. Virgin Islands

*Y*ou may be able to find pigeon peas at your local specialty of health food store. If not, cooked black-eyed peas make a good substitute.

2 tablespoons balsamic vinegar
1/2 cup rice vinegar
2 garlic cloves, crushed
1/3 cup olive oil
2 cups cooked spiral, multi-colored noodles, drained
1 1/2 cup baby carrots
1 roasted red pepper, peeled and chopped
1 cup pigeon peas, cooked or black-eyed beans
1 tablespoon butter
1 shallot, minced
1/4 cup fresh basil, chopped
1/4 cup fresh parsley, chopped
1/2 cup plain breadcrumbs

Toss the vinegars, one garlic clove, and the olive oil into the noodles, carrots, roasted pepper, peas and refrigerate.

Melt the butter in a small sauté pan along with the remaining garlic clove and the shallot. Add the fresh basil and parsley, cooking for one minute. Toss in the breadcrumbs and toast until golden.

Serve the breadcrumb topping hot over the chilled pasta salad.

YIELD: 4 servings

Island Speak: Twin City Translation: St. Croix, U.S. Virgin Islands

Mesclun Salad with Jalapeno Orange Cream
British Virgin Islands

The jalapeno orange cream can also be used with anything from swordfish to filet mignon.

Sauce:
1/4 cup sour cream
3 tablespoons chopped jalapeno peppers (these are the kind found in the supermarket in a jar)
3 tablespoons minced onion
1 clove garlic crushed
2 tablespoons orange juice concentrate
1-tablespoon fresh zest of orange
2 tablespoons honey
5 cups mesclun greens
2 tablespoons fresh basil
1/4 cup fresh cilantro
3 tablespoons minced green onions
2 tangerines, sectioned and seeded

Whirl all the ingredients for the sauce in a blender until pureed smooth.

Toss the greens, with the sauce, onions, basil and cilantro. Garnish with the tangerine slices.

YIELD: 2 servings

Spinach, Onion and Blood Orange Salad with Kumquat Dressing

Grand Cayman

Kumquats are actually a bitter citrus fruit the size of a small egg.

Dressing:
4 kumquats, cut in half and seeded
1/4 cup sour cream
2 tablespoons whipping cream
2 tablespoons granulated sugar
1-teaspoon fresh grated ginger
1/2 teaspoon ground cardamom
1-tablespoon blood orange juice
1/2 teaspoon cayenne pepper
3 tablespoons water

4 cups baby spinach leaves, washed and drained
1 large red onion, thinly sliced
2 blood oranges, peeled, sectioned and chopped (reserve one tablespoon of the blood orange juice for the dressing)
Alfalfa sprouts

Boil the kumquats for 5 minutes and drain. Combine with all other dressing ingredients in a blender and refrigerate.

In a large salad bowl, toss the spinach, onion and blood oranges. Pour the dressing over the top and garnish with alfalfa sprouts.

YIELD: Serves 4

Black Bean, Citrus and Shrimp Salad
Miami

I like to serve this on truly hot summer days, when everyone is hungry and requires cooling down.

1/4 cup olive oil
Juice of three limes
Zest of one lime
2 cloves garlic, crushed
Black beans
1/4 cup chives, chopped
1 pound cooked and peeled shrimp
1 large pink grapefruit, peeled, sectioned and seeded
2 navel oranges, peeled and sectioned
1 Ugli fruit (a cross between a tangerine and grapefruit) peeled and sectioned
Salt and fresh cracked pepper to taste
4 ounces shaved Parmesan curls

Combine the olive oil, limejuice, zest, and garlic in a small bowl.

In a large bowl, combine the beans, chives, shrimp, and citrus fruit. Pour the dressing over the top. Marinate overnight in the refrigerator.

Before serving top with Parmesan. Season with salt and pepper.

YIELD: 4 servings

Bahamian Grilled Tuna and Asparagus Salad
Nassau

Make the asparagus the night before and marinate for peak flavor.

1-pound asparagus spears
1/4 cup extra virgin olive oil
2 garlic cloves crushed
1/4 cup cider vinegar
Juice and zest of one lemon
1-teaspoon coriander
1-tablespoon olive oil
1-tablespoon fresh rosemary
1-teaspoon sea salt
2 one-inch tuna steaks
olive oil for rubbing tuna
4 cups romaine leaves, washed and torn
1/4 cup fresh cilantro
1-cup seedless green grapes
2 hard-boiled eggs, shelled and quartered
1-tablespoon fresh cracked pepper

Cut off the tough ends of the asparagus and discard. Chop into two inch pieces. Steam until just barely tender.

To make the marinade, combine the 1/2 cup olive oil, garlic, vinegar, coriander, lemon juice and zest in a small bowl. Pour over the asparagus and refrigerate.

Preheat a barbecue grill on high. Rub the tuna steaks with the olive oil, rosemary, and salt. Grill the tuna until slightly blackened on each side. Remember the style of tuna these days is rare in the center. If you don't care for this, lower the heat and cook until desired.

Toss the romaine with the asparagus. Divide between two plates and place one tuna steak on top of each salad. Garnish with cilantro, grapes, and hard-boiled eggs. Season with salt and pepper.

YIELD: 2 servings

Did you know?: Tuna are grouped into several species. The most common are blue fin tuna, which is the largest tuna weighing between 220 and 2,000 pounds up to 13 feet long and has a reddish brown meat with an intense taste. The albacore tuna weighs around 100 plus pounds and is up to 40 inches long. The meat is very light in color and mild. The bonito is the smallest, usually less than 20 inches weighing in less than 5 pounds. The Japanese dry and store the flakes. Very high in protein.

Purchasing: Tuna may be purchased canned, but many recipes now call for fresh steaks, which may be purchased at the grocery. Choose firm steaks with no overly fishy smell.

Tip: Poach tuna for 10 minutes before cooking.

Curried Egg Salad in Tomato Shells

St. Martin

Here's a good idea for all those wonderful summer tomatoes from the garden. Even my very fussy uncle enjoyed this recipe and asked for seconds!

8 large hard-boiled eggs
1/4 cup minced green onions
1/4 cup crushed pecans
1/4 cup currants
1-tablespoon fresh cracked black pepper
1/2 cup mayonnaise
1 1/2 tablespoons curry powder
1 tablespoon mango chutney
Salt to taste
6 large red ripe tomatoes

Coarsely chop the eggs and place into a medium bowl. Add the onions, pecans, currants and black pepper. Mix the mayonnaise separately with the curry powder and chutney. Stir into the egg mixture. Chill.

Cut the tops off the tomatoes and scoop out the seeds. Fill with the egg salad. Season with salt and pepper.

YIELD: 6 servings

Cucumber and Crab Carnival

St. Croix, U.S. Virgin Islands

Lobster may be successfully substituted for the crab. Wonderful for Sunday champagne brunches.

1-cup plain yogurt
1/4 sour cream
2 garlic cloves crushed
Juice of two lemons
2 large cucumbers, thinly sliced
1/3 cup minced green onion
1 pound lump crabmeat
12 endive leaves
Fresh parsley
Salt and pepper to taste

In a small bowl, combine the yogurt, sour cream, garlic and lemon juice.

In another bowl, toss the cucumber and onion with the dressing. Fold in the crabmeat. Chill.

Scoop onto the endive leaves and garnish with parsley. Season with salt and pepper.

YIELD: Enough for 4

Minted Zucchini and Orange Salad

Miami

This salad goes nicely with cold poached salmon and a crisp Chardonnay. Make two to three hours ahead of time to chill and mingle the flavors.

4 tablespoons extra-virgin olive oil
2 tablespoons fresh lemon juice
Salt and pepper to taste
2 large zucchini or 3 medium
1/4 cup fresh mint leaves, finely chopped
1 orange, peeled and sectioned
1/4 cup chopped walnuts

In a small bowl, quickly whisk oil, lemon juice, salt, and pepper.

Shred the zucchini using a food processor. In a large bowl, toss the mint with the zucchini. Chop orange sections and add to zucchini along with the walnuts. Slowly pour the vinaigrette over salad and gently toss.

Yield: 4 servings

Grilled Eggplant and Corn Salad with Chipolte Mayonnaise

Mazatlan

3 tablespoons olive oil
1 large eggplant, sliced in 3/8 inch slices
1 red bell pepper, seeded and cut in 1/2 inch strips
1 medium yellow onion, cut in half and sliced lengthwise
3 ears of corn
1/3-cup mayonnaise
1/3-cup low-fat plain yogurt
1 cans chipolata in sauce, pureed
1/2 teaspoon ground cumin
2 tablespoons fresh chopped cilantro
Salt and pepper to taste

Brush with oil the eggplant, red pepper, onion, and corn. Grill over medium heat until slightly charred, about 10 to 15 minutes. Remove from grill, transfer to a glass bowl or plate, allow cooling.

In a small bowl, combine the mayonnaise, yogurt, chipolata in sauce, cilantro, and cumin. Add salt and pepper to taste.

With a sharp knife, remove corn kernels from cob. Peel skin from red pepper slices. Toss vegetables lightly and stir in dressing. Chill thoroughly.

Yield: 2 for salad or 4 as a side dish

Did you know?: Pineapples do not grow on trees, they are a bromeliad. Columbus discovered it on his voyage to Guadeloupe in 1493. The Spanish and Portuguese brought it to Asia. Coming from the Spanish word pina because it resembled a pinecone, the English named it pineapple. The fruit is deep yellow and sweet, while the skin is very rough, inedible and gold to brown in color. Fruits weigh between three and nine pounds. Pineapple contains an enzyme called bromelin, a meat tenderizer. Good source of vitamin C, potassium, magnesium and folic acid.

Purchasing: Choose weighty fruits and smell the base, it should be aromatic, and not too strong, which indicates rotting. Thump the fruit, it should sound solid, a hollow sound may be because of dried out fruit. Watch out for soft spots or black marks.

Storing: Unripe fruit will ripen after several days at room temperature. Refrigerate unripe fruit for several days.

Grilled Pineapple, Avocado and Onion Salad

St. Martin

St. Martin has some truly fabulous restaurants on both the French and Dutch side. It's actually quite easy to put on the weight there. This light salad bursts with a profusion of flavors.

1/2 medium fresh pineapple, peeled, cored and cut in 1/2 inch slices
1 1/2 tablespoons extra-virgin olive oil

Dressing:
Juice of 3 limes
1/4 cup extra-virgin olive oil
1 small Serrano pepper, seeded and minced
1-teaspoon honey
Dash of cinnamon
Salt to taste

1 large red onion
4 large avocados
Juice of one lime

Brush the pineapple with olive oil and grill until slightly charred. Remove from grill and cool in refrigerator.

Combine dressing ingredients in a small bowl and stir.

Quarter avocados lengthwise and peel. Drizzle limejuice over avocado to prevent browning. Cut onion in half and slice thinly lengthwise to form strips. Cut pineapple rings in quarters. Arrange avocado slices on a pretty platter along with onion and pineapple. Stir dressing and pour evenly over salad.

Yield: 4 servings

Tip: Grill pineapple a day ahead to allow thorough chilling.

Mango and Proscuitto with Fresh Basil and Feta

St. Martin

This is a delightful twist on a the traditional melon and proscuitto. I found this recipe on one of my many sojourns to St. Martin.

1/4 cup olive oil
1/3 cup fresh basil leaves, chopped
juice of one lemon
salt and pepper to taste
1/4 cup crumbled feta
3 tablespoons walnuts, crushed
2 large ripe, yet firm mangoes
1/2 pound thinly sliced proscuitto

Puree olive oil and basil in blender. Combine olive oil mixture, lemon juice, salt and pepper in small bowl. Stir in feta and walnuts; allow to marinate in the refrigerator.

Peel mangoes by cutting through skin with knife making 4 cuts top to bottom. Grab hold of skin and peel downward. Cut slices, being careful of large pit.

Arrange mango onto 4 plates and arrange proscuitto over the top. Spoon dressing over the top.

Yield: 4 servings

Tropical Citrus and Rice Salad

Dominica

Refreshing on hot summer days.

1 medium carrot
1 small zucchini
1/2 pink grapefruit, peeled, sectioned, seeded
1 medium orange, peeled, sectioned, seeded
2 scallions, chopped
1 stalk celery, chopped
2 tablespoons fresh cilantro, chopped
2 cups cooked white or fragrant basmati rice

Dressing:

Juice of two limes
1/4 cup olive oil
1 clove garlic, crushed
1 tablespoon Cointreau Mango Chutney
1-teaspoon hot pepper flakes
2 tablespoons water
Salt and pepper to taste

Shred the carrot and zucchini in a food processor. Chop grapefruit and orange sections, toss with zucchini mix, scallion, celery and cilantro. Carefully fold in the rice. Cool for 2 hours in the refrigerator.

Combine dressing ingredients in a small bowl and chill as well.

Drizzle dressing over rice mixture and serve at once.

Yield: 4 servings

Tip

*Be sure to carefully read each recipe to check for pre-chilled ingredients. This will save inordinate amounts of preparation time.

*Have all ingredients properly assembled and prepared before beginning recipe.

*For accuracy measure liquids in see-through measuring cups.

*Sanitize all fruits and vegetables in a large glass bowl or clean sink using one teaspoon bleach to one gallon of water. Soak for 10 minutes. Do this to fruits that need peeling such as pineapple, kiwi, mango, papaya etc. so as not to transfer bacteria to fruit upon cutting. Rinse extremely well to remove all traces of bleach.

Bahamian Chef's Salad

Freeport, Nassau

Perhaps I am dating myself, but I remember when a Chef's Salad was the most popular item on the menu. With the trend veering away from high calorie dressings and processed meat, this salad is healthful alternative to all that cholesterol.

2 medium carrots, peeled
1 small zucchini
1 small head Romaine lettuce, washed, dried and torn into bite-size pieces
2 cups baby spinach leaves, washed and dried
2 scallions, chopped
1/4 mayonnaise
1/2 teaspoon dried or 1 teaspoon fresh dill
1/2 teaspoon cayenne pepper
1 pound cooked lobster meat
8 asparagus spears, lightly steamed
1 pound ripe cherry tomatoes

dressing:
1/3 cup extra-virgin olive oil
1 garlic clove, crushed
1/2 teaspoon each:
fresh basil
marjoram
thyme
4 tablespoons white Balsamic vinegar
3 tablespoons water
1/2 cup grated Parmigiano-Reggiano
salt and pepper to taste

Put the carrot and zucchini through a food processor and shred. Toss the romaine, spinach, zucchini mix, and scallions in a very large bowl. Set aside in refrigerator.
Mix mayonnaise, dill and cayenne pepper in medium bowl. Toss in lobster chunks and thoroughly coat. Set aside in refrigerator.
To make dressing combine all ingredients in a small bowl.
Fold in lobster with salad mixture. Top with tomatoes and asparagus. Drizzle dressing over the top.

Yield: 4 servings

Starters and
Beginners

Conch Fritters

When I moved to St. Thomas, I tasted conch for the first time in the form of a delightfully spicy stew at a restaurant called Gracy's in downtown Charlotte Amalie. Conch is available stateside in the larger cities, and your local fish market may be able to special order it for you.

Kill Devil Conch Fritters

St. Thomas, U.S. Virgin Islands

St. Thomas is known as the shopping capitol of the Caribbean.

1 small boiled potato, peeled and mashed
1 stalk celery, minced
1 small carrot, grated
2 garlic cloves, crushed and minced
1 teaspoon thyme
1 medium onion, minced
1 small red bell pepper, well chopped
1 to 2 habanero peppers, seeded and minced
2 cups all-purpose flour
1 1/2 teaspoon baking powder
1 cup stale beer
1 1/2 pounds of conch, pounded and sent through a food processor
oil for frying
Cointreau Mango Chutney
Hot sauce

In a large bowl, combine the potato, celery, carrot, garlic, thyme, onion and peppers. Gradually stir in the flour, baking powder, then slowly pour in the beer, adding in the ground conch. Remember if you do not pound the conch long enough or send it through the grinder, it will be extremely tough.

In a skillet with tall sides, heat the oil. Drop the batter in by large tablespoonfuls and fry until golden. Drain on white paper towels and serve while still hot with chutney and hot sauce.

Yield: 36 to 40 fritters

Island-Style Guacamole
Virgin Islands

I'll never forget how upset my father-in-law was when he thought he finally lost his last avocado tree after Hurricane Marilyn in 1995.. . . Virgin Islanders love their avocados. This excellent dip is a bit on the fiery side, but keeps its bright color a little longer due to all the fresh citrus juice.

3 large ripe avocados
2 tablespoons fresh lime juice
2 tablespoons fresh lemon juice
2 tablespoons orange juice
1 large ripe tomato, chopped
1 medium yellow onion, minced
1 scotch bonnet, seeded and minced
1/4 cup tinned corn kernels, drained
1 tablespoon chili powder
1 teaspoon minced garlic

Peel and pit the avocado. Coarsely chop and mash with the three citrus juices. Fold in the onion, tomato, scotch bonnet, and corn. Add the garlic and chili powder. Goes well with low or non-fat chips as the high oil content of the avocados contribute a good deal of flavor. Of course, regular corn chips are equally delicious, especially when served with an ice-cold beer.

Yield: enough for 6

Did you know? Avocados are also called alligator pears. The fruit grows on trees up to 65 feet in height, but very fragile during tropical storms. The Hass avocado has a pebbly and rough brown or black skin and is slightly smaller than the Fuerte, Zutano or Bacon avocados. These have a bright green, glossy skin. The skin cannot be eaten. Avocados have a beneficial high fat content with a rich, nutty, buttery and creamy meat with a large pit. Good source of potassium, folic acid, B6, magnesium, pantothenic acid, vitamin C, and zinc.
Purchasing: Choose weighty avocados, without spots, that give a little when pressed.
Storing: Leave at room temperature to ripen. Ripe fruit keeps for several days in the refrigerator.

Trinidadian Doubles

St. Croix, U.S. Virgin Islands

I love East Indian food. As we learned earlier, the East Indians traveled to the Caribbean as indentured servants after slavery was abolished and brought their delightfully aromatic and alternatingly hot cuisine with them. They say that Doubles are exclusive to Trinidad, but I had them in St. Croix not too long ago at this little roadside roti shack.

Filling:
1/2 teaspoon ground turmeric
1/2 teaspoon ground cumin
1/2 teaspoon ground coriander
1/4 teaspoon fenugreek
1/4 teaspoon ground cloves
1/4 teaspoon allspice
1/2 teaspoon cinnamon
2 tablespoons ghee, or clarified butter
1 habanero pepper, seeded and minced
2 teaspoons crushed garlic
1 1/2 tablespoon fresh ground ginger
1 large onion, minced
1 16-ounce can chickpeas, drained
water

to make bread:
1/2 cup all-purpose flour
1/4 cup finely ground cornmeal
3/4 cup split pea flour (available from Indian groceries or the healthfood store)
3 teaspoons baking powder
1/4 cup warm water
vegetable oil for frying

Filling:

Put all the spices in a large skillet with tall sides. Slowly heat and roast the spices. They will give off a pleasant aroma and darken slightly. Add ghee, habanero, garlic, ginger and the onion. Cook until the onion is clear.

Add one cup water to skillet and the chickpeas. Cook for 20 minutes and then mash the chickpeas with a potato masher. Add water as needed.

Bread: Put all ingredients in a large bowl and combine. Knead slightly on floured surface, return to bowl and cover for 45 minutes in a warm place to rise.

Scoop up about 2 tablespoons of the dough and roll to about 1/4 inch thickness. Fry in the oil until golden. Drain on paper towels.

Make sandwiches with the chickpea filling, hence the name doubles, i.e. top and bottom.

Yield: approximately 6 servings

Cayman Turtles

Grand Cayman

On this fourth and final voyage, Columbus discovered the Caymans in 1503. Actually until I researched this book, I had completely forgotten that Columbus made so many trips or had discovered so many islands. He called the islands "Las Tortugas" i.e. The Turtles. There must also have been a good many large lizards as the islands became the Caymans due to the Carib Indian word for crocodile. I like to serve this cute appetizer at parties where I am not quite sure how spicy the guests prefer their food.

2/3 cup all-purpose flour
2 tablespoons butter
1 cup extra-sharp cheddar. Grated
1 3 ounce package cream cheese
2 tablespoons minced pimentos
1/2 teaspoon minced garlic
1 tablespoon minced onion
1 small jar pimento stuffed olives
96 walnut halves
1 tablespoon Tabasco sauce

Preheat oven to 375 degrees.

In a medium bowl, combine all ingredients except olives and walnuts. Scoop up 1 tablespoon of the dough and stuff an olive in the center of the dough. Stick 4 walnut halves on the bottom of the dough to resemble feet.

Arrange on non-stick cookie sheet and bake for 15 minutes until golden.

Yield: 24 Tortugas

Havana Sweet Potato Chips

Cuba

These eye-catching chips rank high on the nutritional scale—lots of vitamin A. Why not serve choice sweet potato chips instead of corn chips at your next cocktail party?

4 pounds sweet potatoes, well scrubbed
1 quart canola oil, for frying
sea salt and fresh ground pepper to taste

With a large heavy knife, slice the sweet potatoes as thinly as possible. Heat the oil to 400 degrees. Drop the sweet potatoes in the hot oil and fry for about 1 minute. Drain on white paper towels

Season with salt and pepper to taste.

Yield: 6 servings

Island Speak: Irie, mee son. Translation: I agree, my friend.

Jamaican Stamp and Go

Jamaica

In Colonial days, these delectable codfish cakes were sold wrapped in paper and stamped paid. Before refrigeration, the only means to preserve fish and meat was to use salt. In the Virgin Islands, cod is called Saltfish.

1 pound salt fish
2 tablespoon butter
1 small onion minced
1/2 teaspoon minced garlic
1 small red bell pepper, minced
1 small green bell pepper, minced
1/2 habanero pepper, seeded and minced
1 cup all-purpose flour
1 cup soft white breadcrumbs
2 eggs, beaten
1 1/2 teaspoon baking powder
vegetable oil for frying
cayenne pepper
salt and pepper to taste

To remove some of the salt from the fish, soak it in water in the refrigerator for 12 hours. Try to change the water several times. The more often the water is changed, the less salty the fish will be.

In a large saucepan, bring the water and cod to a boil and reduce heat, simmering for 15 minutes. Drain the fish and flake as you would a can of tuna fish.

Heat the butter and sauté the onion, garlic and peppers until onions are clear. Remove from heat.

In a glass bowl, combine the flour, breadcrumbs, baking powder and eggs. Fold in the onion mixture and fish.

In a large skillet with tall sides and a lid, heat the oil. Drop by heaping tablespoonfuls into the oil. Fry until truly golden and drain on paper towels. Season with salt, pepper and a dash of cayenne.

Yield: 4 servings

Onion and Mango-Orange Cream Cheese Spread on Garlic Rounds
British Virgin Islands

This delightful spread has extra 'heat' with the addition of the West Indian scotch bonnet pepper. Adjust the fire by adding or subtracting the amount of pepper.

1 loaf French bread
1/4 butter, softened
1 tablespoon garlic

2 tablespoons olive oil
2 large red onions
1 teaspoon crushed garlic
1 scotch bonnet pepper
1/2 cucumber, peeled and finely chopped
1 teaspoon fresh grated ginger
1 cup distilled vinegar
1/2 cup sugar
3 oranges, peeled, seeded and chopped
2 8 ounce packages cream cheese at room temperature
1/3 cup walnuts, chopped
2/3 cup fresh chopped mango
1/2 teaspoon cardamom
dash of cinnamon
1 tablespoon honey
1 tablespoon limejuice

Sauté the onion, garlic, pepper, cucumber, and 1/2 teaspoon of the ginger in the olive oil until the onion is clear.

In a medium sauce pan, bring the vinegar and sugar to a boil. Add the oranges and onion mixture. Cook approximately 30 minutes over medium heat, stirring frequently. Allow cooling to room temperature.

Slice the French bread into 1/2 inch slices. Mix the garlic with the 1/2 cup butter and spread each round. Toast in the oven at 350 degrees until golden. Allow to dry out on rack.

In a large glass bowl cream together the cream cheese, walnuts, mango, and orange/onion mixture. Stir in spices, honey, remaining 1/2 teaspoon ginger and limejuice. Chill for 3 to 4 hours.

Spread 1 tablespoon of the spread on each garlic round.

Yield: 24 appetizers

Crab and Potato Cakes
Grand Cayman

When I traveled to Grand Cayman for a photography assignment, we drove down a stretch of road that was literally covered with thousands of huge land crabs in all colors of orange, yellow, brown and black. My husband needed a photo of this, so I got out of the car and walked in the midst of them. There were so many we had to shoo them away from the car so we could drive. The natives will catch these giant land crabs and feed them bread and cornmeal for a week to purge them. This recipe is quick to make if you have leftover mashed potatoes on hand.

1 yellow onion, minced
1 stalk celery, minced
1 teaspoon crushed garlic
1/2 red bell pepper, diced finely
1 tablespoon butter
2 cups mashed potatoes
2 tins lump crab meat, flaked (fresh is better)
2 eggs, beaten
1/2 cup seasoned breadcrumbs
vegetable oil for frying

Sauté the onion, celery, garlic and pepper in the butter.

In a large bowl, flake the crab. Combine with the potato, onion mixture, and all other ingredients except oil.

Heat the oil in a skillet and drop the dough by large tablespoonfuls into the oil. Fry until golden and drain on white paper towels.

Season to taste with salt and pepper and serve hot.

Yield: 12 to 16 cakes

Coconut Shrimp Fritters with Passionfruit Sauce

St. Vincent and the Grenadines

Passionfruit Sauce:
1 tablespoon butter
3 tablespoons minced onion
1 tablespoon cornstarch, sifted
1/4 cup tablespoons passionfruit liqueur
1 tablespoon vinegar
3 tablespoons brown sugar
1/2 teaspoon instant chicken bouillon granules
2 passionfruit, seeded and pulp removed

fritters:
1 cup all-purpose flour
1 1/2 teaspoons baking powder
1/4 cup melted butter
1 teaspoon crushed garlic
hot pepper sauce to taste
1 egg, beaten
1 stalk celery, minced
1 medium yellow onion, minced
1 grated carrot
1/2 teaspoon fresh grated ginger
2 tablespoons fresh basil, chopped
2/3 cup sweetened cream of coconut
1/2 cup plain breadcrumbs
2/3 cup grated coconut
2 pounds cooked, chopped shrimp
water
vegetable oil for frying

Sauce: in a medium saucepan, sauté the onions in the butter until soft. In another small container, quickly whisk in the cornstarch with the liqueur and the vinegar until no lumps remain. Pour into the sauté pan, adding the sugar, bouillon, and fruit pulp.

Continue to cook until bubbly and thickened. Remove from heat and cool 15 minutes. Pour into a blender or food processor to puree.

Fritters: sift the baking powder together with the flour in a bowl. In another bowl, combine the butter, garlic, hot pepper sauce, egg, celery, onion, carrot, ginger, basil and cream of coconut. Stir in the breadcrumbs, grated coconut and shrimp. Gradually stir in the flour and add enough water as necessary to make a good batter.

Drop by large tablespoonfuls in the heated oil, cooking until golden. Drain on plain white paper towels. Serve with Passionfruit Sauce.

Yield: 6 servings

Jalapeno, Papaya and Edam Wedges

St. Maarten

Either Gouda or Edam cheese may be used successfully in this delicious biscuit recipe. We buy giant wheels of this Holland cheese while visiting St. Maarten, Dutch West Indies. The most marvelous melted cheese sandwiches can be had at the airport. Cut out the dough with cookie cutters and serve with plenty of cocktails to cool the fire.

1/2 cup minced fresh papaya
1/4 teaspoon nutmeg
1 cup Gouda or Edam cheese, grated
3 tablespoons chopped jalapeno peppers
3 teaspoons baking powder
2 cups all-purpose flour
1/3 cup vegetable shortening
1/4 cup evaporated milk
1/2 cup milk

Preheat oven to 450 degrees and use a non-stick baking sheet.

In a small bowl, combine papaya, nutmeg, cheese, and jalapeno peppers and set aside.

In large heavy bowl, sift together the baking powder and flour. Using a pastry blender or two knives, cut in the shortening until crumbly. Fold in the papaya mixture. Add milks and form into a dough.

On a floured surface, knead the dough about 10 times. Cut out rounds with a small cookie or biscuit cutter.

Bake 10 to 12 minutes until golden. Serve hot.

Yield: 12 biscuits

Curried Potato and Corn Strudel
Nevis

This different strudel can be successfully served as either an appetizer or a main dish.

Filling:
1 teaspoon turmeric
1/2 teaspoon cumin
1/4 teaspoon fenugreek
1/2 teaspoon coriander
1/2 teaspoon fresh grated pepper
1/4 teaspoon cinnamon
1 large onion, minced
1/2 teaspoon crushed garlic
1/2 teaspoon fresh grated ginger
2 tablespoons butter
2 large potatoes, peeled and grated

10 sheets phyllo dough
1/2 cup, plus 2 tablespoons melted butter
1/3 cup breadcrumbs

1/3 cup mango chutney
water

Preheat oven to 350 degrees.

In a small pan, roast the turmeric, cumin, foenugreek, coriander, pepper, and cinnamon until a pleasant aroma is emitted and the spices darken slightly. Remove from heat.

In a large sauce pan, sauté the onion, garlic, and ginger in the butter. Add the water and spices, stirring well. Spoon in the grated potatoes and cook until soft, about 10 to 12 minutes.

Lightly grease a baking sheet and or use a non-stick sheet. Unfold the phyllo sheets and cover with a damp dish towel.

Place 1 sheet of the phyllo on a piece of waxed paper. Using a pastry brush, brush each sheet gently with the melted butter and sprinkle with bread-crumbs. Repeat with remaining sheets.

Spread the mango chutney on top of the last remaining sheet. Spoon the filling onto the pastry, leaving 2 1/2 inch margins around the edge. Start at long end and roll strudel up. It's easier to use the waxed paper. With wet fingers, seal edges shut.

Bake approximately 25 minutes until golden.

Yield: 6 main course servings or 12 appetizers

Island Speak: Debil temp bu he no fawc. Translation: Temptation is always there, but you don't have to give in to it.

Caribbean Pizza
St. Thomas, U.S. Virgin Islands

Bring back exotic island memories with this fresh-tasting pizza with papaya, shrimp, peppery Boursin and creamy ricotta. Cut into slender wedges for appetizers.

Crust:
1 teaspoon active dry yeast
1/2 cup warm water
1 1/2 cups all-purpose flour
1/2 teaspoon salt
1 tablespoon olive oil

Topping:
1 package Boursin cheese (peppery kind)
3/4 cup Ricotta cheese
1/2 teaspoon crushed garlic
2/3 cup papaya, peeled and finely diced
1 tablespoon fresh oregano
1 cup baby shrimp, cooked and peeled
2/3 cup shredded Provolone
2/3 cup shredded Mozzarella

Using a large bowl, dissolve the yeast in the warm water. Allow to stand for 10 minutes.

Sift together the flour and salt. Using an electric beater, mix in 1/2 cup at a time of the flour. Finally, using a spoon mix in the remainder of the flour, working in oil.

Turn out onto a floured surface and knead for 6 to 8 minutes. The dough should be elastic. Cover and leave in a warm place for about an hour.

Preheat oven to 375 degrees. Punch down dough and spread into a greased 9 to 10 inch pan. Bake for 15 minutes and remove from oven.

Increase heat of oven to 425 degrees.

To make filling, cream together the Boursin and the Ricotta cheese along with the garlic, papaya and oregano. Spread over the crust evenly. Distribute the shrimp over the creamed cheeses; sprinkle the Provolone and Mozzarella over the top.

Bake until cheese is bubbly and crust lightly browned.

Yield: 4 dinner servings
12 appetizer servings

Savory Starfruit-Stuffed Cherry Tomatoes
Martinique

Choose cherry tomatoes that are slightly firm, it will make scooping out the centers that much easier.

2 dozen cherry tomatoes
1 8 ounce package cream cheese
1/2 cup Starfruit-Walnut Chutney

Carefully slice the tops off the cherry tomatoes, being careful not to take too much off. Using a small scoop take out the seeds. Drain tomatoes upside down on plain white paper towels.

In a small bowl, cream together the cream cheese and the Starfruit-Walnut Chutney. Using a pastry bag with a large opening, fill the tomatoes. Chill for 4 hours or overnight.

Yield: 24 appetizers

Did you know? Starfruit or Carambola is a native of Ceylon? The fruit is between 2 and 5 inches in diameter and resembles a star when cut crosswise. Light yellow in color, it has a tart flavor
Purchasing: Choose unblemished light yellow fruits, with a pleasant perfume.
Storing: Ripe Carambolas will store up to 2 weeks in the refrigerator.
Preparation: Eat this fruit raw or cooked.

Virgin Island Spicy Meat Pates
St. Thomas, U.S. Virgin Islands

Whenever my family and I manage to get to the airport early in St. Thomas, we do one of two things. We buy wonderfully aromatic and spicy meat pates from local roadside stands or eat at a nearby beach restaurant.

Pastry:
2 cups all-purpose flour
1/2 teaspoon salt
1/2 cup butter, chilled
1 teaspoon fresh ground pepper
5 tablespoons cold water

Filling:
1 pound extra-lean ground beef
1 large yellow onion, minced
1 large green bell pepper, minced
1/2 to 1 habanero pepper, seeded and minced
1/2 cup unseasoned breadcrumbs
1/4 cup pimento-stuffed green olives, minced
6 ounces of canned tomatoes, drained and chopped
4 tablespoons apple cider vinegar
1 teaspoon crushed oregano
1/2 teaspoon allspice
salt and pepper to taste
1 cup sharp grated cheddar cheese

Sift the flour, salt, and pepper into a large bowl. Using two knives or a pastry cutter, cut the butter into the flour until coarse crumbs form. Work in the water and chill in the refrigerator for 1 hour.

In a large skillet, cook the meat, onions, garlic and peppers. Drain and rinse the meat in a colander using hot water. Most of the fat and the calories will run off, leaving all of the flavor.

Stir in breadcrumbs, olives, tomatoes, vinegar, herbs, and spices.

Preheat oven to 425 degrees. On a well-floured surface, roll out the dough

111

and cut out 4 inch circles. Spoon filling into the centers, top with grated cheese and pinch shut with wet fingers.

Bake on lightly greased baking sheet until golden, about 15 minutes.

Yield: 16 to 20 appetizers

Breads,
Fritters
and Sides

Viola's Corn and Hazelnut Spoon Bread
St. Vincent

The Grenadines are small islands which provide a secluded refuge for the rich and famous. This sweet and nutty cornbread compliments any of the fiery habanero or Jerk dishes.

1/2 cup hazelnuts
1 cup yellow cornmeal
2 cups boiling water
1 1/2 cups fresh corn kernels
1 cup milk
1/4 cup sour cream
3 tablespoons butter
1/2 teaspoon vanilla
2 large eggs, beaten
1/2 teaspoon salt
1 tablespoon granulated sugar
1 1/2 teaspoons baking powder
1/2 teaspoon baking soda
4 egg whites
2 tablespoons brown sugar
1/2 teaspoon cinnamon
1/4 cup Hazelnut liqueur

Preheat oven to 350∞.

Roast hazelnuts on a cookie sheet for 15 minutes. Remove from oven and place upon a clean dish towel once cool. Rub nuts with towel to remove skins and grind finely in a food processor. Set aside.

In a large bowl combine the boiling water with the cornmeal, stir and set aside.

In a food processor place 1 cup of the fresh corn kernels along with the milk, sour cream, butter, vanilla, eggs, salt and granulated sugar. Puree and pour into bowl with cornmeal, stir. Fold in the remaining fresh corn kernels along with the baking powder and soda.

Beat the egg whites until peaks have formed and carefully fold into batter. Set aside. Batter will puff up slightly.

In a small bowl, combine the brown sugar, ground hazelnuts, cinnamon, and the liqueur.

Spoon the batter into a buttered deep glass baking dish, sprinkle hazelnut topping over batter.

Bake for 30 minutes until golden.

Yield: 6 servings

Banana Daiquiri Bread
Turks and Caicos

Caicos comes from the Spanish word cayos meaning string of islands. Yes, you guessed it—time to pull out the old rum bottle again. Did you ever put it away?

There's this fancy coffee shop in St. Thomas that makes the most incredible banana bread. The owner was rather territorial with his recipe, but I had the good fortune to later hire one of his employees who finally passed it on to me.

butter
1 1/4 cups granulated sugar
1/4 cup butter, melted
1 tablespoons Cointreau
3 tablespoons dark rum
2 cups mashed bananas
1/2 cup milk
2 eggs beaten
2 1/4 cups all-purpose flour
1/2 teaspoon baking powder
1/2 teaspoon baking soda
1/4 teaspoon cinnamon
1/2 teaspoon salt

Preheat oven to 350° and butter a glass loaf dish. Take 1 tablespoon of the flour and lightly coat the bottom and sides of the dish.

In a large bowl using an electric beater combine the sugar and butter. Add the Cointreau, rum, bananas, milk, and eggs.

Sift together all dry ingredients and add to butter mixture. Beat until combined, but do not over beat.

Bake for 1 hour and insert a toothpick to check for doneness. Continue baking until toothpick comes out clean.

Yield: 1 loaf or 8 to 10 servings

Johnny Cakes

St. Thomas, U.S. Virgin Islands

The African slaves originally did not eat bread. Eventually, they somewhat adapted to their owners' bread making and the end result was Johnny Cakes. In Trinidad, these fried dough biscuits are known as "Bakes".

I remember all too well, the countless times our family arrived late for an airport departure. There really was no decent place to obtain a quick breakfast other than this lone vendor with his lunch truck next to the airport. Those Johnny Cakes really hit the spot! Try them with sugar and cinnamon. I like them with a mustard-based Caribbean hot sauce. This recipe is good and basic—so be sure to serve plenty at your next Caribbean fete.

2 cups flour
2 teaspoons baking powder
1/2 teaspoon sea salt
1 tablespoon sugar
1/4 cup vegetable shortening
1/2 cup milk
vegetable oil for deep frying
optional: granulated sugar and cinnamon or hot chili sauce

With a pastry cutter or fork cut the shortening into the sifted dry ingredients. Add just enough milk to moisten. Knead for about 4 or 5 minutes and roll out on a floured surface. Use a round cookie cutter or clean empty glass jar to cut out 2 to 3 inch rounds.

Drop into hot fat and fry until golden. Remove and drain on white paper towels.

Yield: approximately 24 cakes

Sweet Coconut Dumb Bread

St. Croix, U.S. Virgin Islands

This deliciously sweet bread can be found in all the tiny family-run local bakeries on the island. The couple that gave me this recipe owns a bakery just outside of Christiansted and suggested substituting 3 tablespoons of light rum for part of the milk.

1 1/2 teaspoons active yeast
4 tablespoons warm water
2 cups all-purpose flour
dash of nutmeg
1/2 teaspoon cinnamon
1/4 cup butter
1/4 cup granulated sugar
1/4 cup warm milk
1 tablespoon rum
1 teaspoon fresh or dried orange peel
3/4 cup freshly grated coconut
1/4 cup raisins

Dissolve yeast in the warm water and set aside. Sift together all flour, nutmeg and cinnamon. Cream the butter and the sugar and cut into dry ingredients. Slowly add the milk, rum, vanilla, orange peel, coconut, raisins and yeast until a dough is formed.

Knead gently for about 5 minutes on a floured surface. Cover with a clean dish towel and allow to rise until twice its original size.

Punch down dough and place in a greased loaf or bread pan allowing to rise until double again. In the meantime, preheat oven to 350∞.

Place in center of oven being careful not to let the pan touch the sides of the oven and bake for 30 minutes. A toothpick inserted should come out clean.

Carefully turn loaf upside down, removing from pan. Allow to cool on rack.

Yield: Serves 8 to 10

Island Speak: *When hurricane da blow all skin one cula.*
Translation: Everyone shares equally in the devastation of a hurricane.

Gingered Sweet Potato Muffins
Martinique

Named Martinique by Arawak Indians, the island's lush verdant beauty is dotted with hibiscus, wild orchids, anthurium and a rainbow of bougainvillea.

shortening
1 1/2 cups all-purpose flour
1 1/2 tablespoons baking powder
1/2 teaspoon salt
3/4 cup butter
4 eggs, beaten
1 teaspoon freshly grated ginger
1/4 cup firmly packed brown sugar
1/2 cup granulated sugar
1 1/2 cups milk
1 teaspoon vanilla
1 pound sweet potatoes, boiled, peeled and mashed
shortening to grease muffin tins

Preheat oven to 350∞. Use a non-stick muffin tin or grease generously with shortening, as butter will burn.

Sift the flour, baking powder and salt together—set aside. Cream the butter, eggs, ginger and sugars. Cut into the dry ingredients. In a separate bowl, whisk together the egg mixture, milk and vanilla. Gradually stir into the flour mixture. Fold in sweet potatoes, combining well.

Fill the muffin tins about 2/3 full, baking for about 30 minutes until golden. A toothpick should come out clean—do not over bake!

Yield: about a dozen large muffins

Did you know? The Sweet Potato is a tuber native to Central America. Frequently mistaken for a potato, it belongs to the Convolculaceae family with the Morning Glory. Do not confuse this with the yam, which is not as tasty. In the 16th century the sweet potato traveled via the Spanish Conquistadors to the Philippines; Africa, Asia and Indonesia by the Portuguese explorers. The tubers grow on a vine whose leaves are eaten like spinach. There are two primary groups of yams, which include over 400 varieties. The first group has firm dry flesh and the second group has moist insides. High in vitamin A, good source of potassium. Also has vitamin C, B6, riboflavin, copper, pantothenic and folic acid.

Purchasing: Choose firm tubers without fungus, spots or cracks. Do not purchase refrigerated potatoes as this spoils the flavor.

Storage: Do not refrigerate. Keep in cool, dark place with air circulation for 7 to 10 days. After cooking may be refrigerated for up to a week or frozen.

Preparation: The sweet potato will discolor upon peeling, so quickly immerse in cool water to prevent this.

Mango Fritters
Anguilla

Victoria's Secret, Elle and Cosmopolitan have all chosen sheltered Anguilla for their photo shoots.

1/4 cup sugar
1 1/4 cups all-purpose flour
1 1/4 teaspoons baking powder
1/2 teaspoon salt
1/2 teaspoon cinnamon
1/2 teaspoon nutmeg
dash allspice
1 egg
1 teaspoon vanilla
1/4 cup water
2 cups finely chopped mango
1/2 teaspoon freshly grated ginger
vegetable oil for frying
granulated sugar for topping

The amount of water has been reduced by 1/2 in this recipe to account for the plentiful juice from the mango. If additional water is necessary, add by the tablespoon.

Sift the dry ingredients together. Whisk together the egg, vanilla and water and add to the dry ingredients. Fold in the mango and ginger until well moistened.

Drop by large spoonfuls into the hot fat, frying until golden. Drain on paper towels.

Dust with sugar and serve at once.

Yield: 8 servings

Conch Fritters

St. Croix

The island of Dr. Moreau was filmed here.

1 1/2 cups all-purpose flour
1/2 teaspoon salt
2 teaspoons baking powder
1 egg, beaten
3/4 cup milk
1/4 unsweetened coconut milk
1 pound conch meat, pounded and sent through a meat grinder or food processor
2 scallions chopped
4 tablespoons chopped parsley
1 small stalk celery minced
vegetable oil for frying
salt and pepper to taste
habanero hot sauce as a condiment

Sift flour, salt, and baking powder together in a large bowl. Make a well in the center of the flour. Combine the egg and milks and gradually add to flour. Stir until a smooth batter has formed, folding in the ground conch meat and vegetables.

Drop by the spoonful into the hot fat, frying until golden. Season to taste with salt and pepper. Serve with habanero hot sauce.

Yield: 8 servings

Stamp and Go
Jamaica

In the early days, cod was salted as a means of preservation. One can still easily find salted cod in Caribbean grocery stores. In Jamaica the cakes were initially wrapped in paper and stamped "paid"—there of which is derived Stamp and Go.

1/2 pound salt cod
1 cup all-purpose flour
1 teaspoon baking powder
pinch of baking soda
1/2 teaspoon salt
1 egg, beaten
1/2 cup milk
1 teaspoon habanero hot sauce or equally hot chili sauce
1 small onion, finely diced
pinch of dried thyme
salt and freshly ground pepper to taste
vegetable oil for frying

Soak the cod overnight in the refrigerator using a large glass bowl filled with water to remove the salt. Drain and rinse under cold water.

Fill a saucepan with fresh water and simmer the cod for about 20 minutes. Remove the fish and carefully pick and discard the skin and bones. Press any excess water from the fish. Flake fish with a fork and set aside.

Sift the dry ingredients in a large bowl. Combine the egg, milk, and the hot sauce and slowly stir into the flour. Fold in the onion, thyme and flaked cod.

Drop by the spoonful into the hot batter and fry until golden. Drain on white paper towels. Wrap in clean strips from brown paper bags. Season with salt and pepper.

Yield: 24 Stamp and Go

Did you know? Shrimp are small crustaceans that can be found all over the world? They can be found in fresh or salt water at all temperatures and everything in between. Shrimp consist of nine different families and nearly 160 different species. Americans consume nearly 5 million pounds of shrimp annually. The most popular and tasty shrimp is called the pink shrimp, a deep water shrimp.

Shrimp are high in vitamin B12 and niacin.

Purchasing: Buy only firm shrimp that have only a faint fishy smell. Shrimp spoil quickly, so avoid soft, sticky bodies, detached shells, an ammonia smell, which indicates decomposition, or black spots. Steer clear of frozen shrimp that are covered with freezer frost or ice as this spoils the flavor.

Storing: Shrimp are quite perishable, so fresh shrimp for no more than two days in the refrigerator or freeze for one month.

Preparation: Remember that shrimp will lose half of their body weight upon cooking. It is easier to shell slightly frozen shrimp. Shell shrimp by holding the head in one hand and the body with the other hand. Pull on the head. To pull out the vein, slit along the vein with a sharp knife and pull it out in one piece.

Fiery Shrimp and Potato Cakes
St. Maarten, Netherlands Antilles

St. Maarten is Dutch on one side and French (St. Martin) on the other.

1 1/2 cups mashed potatoes
2 tablespoons butter
1 cup grated extra-sharp aged cheddar
1/4 cup all-purpose flour
2 tablespoons freshly chopped parsley
1 tablespoon freshly chopped cilantro
1 egg yolk, beaten
2 medium scallions, chopped
1 medium Serrano or other fiery pepper, minced
2 tablespoons Mango Chutney
1 pound cooked, cleaned shrimp, chopped
salt and pepper
1/2 cup all-purpose flour
1 egg beaten
vegetable oil for frying

In a large bowl combine the mashed potato, butter, cheddar, 1/2 cup flour, parsley, cilantro, egg yolk, scallions, chili pepper, chutney and the shrimp. Salt and pepper to taste. Refrigerate for at least two hours.

Heat the oil in a deep frying pan. Remove the dough from the refrigerator and form into small balls slightly larger than a golf ball, then flatten. Have the beaten egg ready in a small bowl and the 1/2 cup flour on a small plate. Dip each cake into the egg and then dredge in flour.

Deep fry several until golden. Drain on paper towels. Serve hot.

Yield: approximately 12 cakes

Taino Casabe Bread

Santa Domingo

Cassava, a bread made from yucca flour originated with the Taino Indians and is still commonly served today. This low calorie and thin bread is served as an accompaniment to meals.

4 pounds fresh yucca
clean cheese cloth or dish cloth

non-stick frying pan

Fill a kitchen sink 1/2 way with water and 3 tablespoons of bleach. Soak the yucca on all sides with the bleach. Drain and rinse very well. This will disinfect the vegetable from contaminants.

Using a good sharp potato peeler, scrape off the brown skin. One can use a grater for the yucca, but I have found it easier to puree in the food processor.

Place the puree in the cheese cloth and weigh down with clean rocks or even a cement block. This will squeeze out the excess water.

Heat the frying pan until very hot. Place approximately 1 cup of the still moist cassava flour on the bottom of the pan, about 1/8 inch thick. Cook until dry— about 5 minutes and turn over.

Store in airtight sealed container for up to a week.

Yield: 6 large cakes

Virgin Island Beef Pates

St. Thomas, U.S. Virgin Islands

These spicy hot meat turnovers are a lunch and at times a breakfast staple in the Virgin Islands. Delicious served hot with ice-cold beer.

Pastry:
4 cups sifted all-purpose flour
1 teaspoon salt
1 1/2 teaspoons turmeric
3/4 cup vegetable shortening
1/3 cup ice water

filling:
1 1/2 tablespoons olive oil
1 small onion, minced
1 clove garlic, minced
1 medium habanero pepper, seeded and minced
1 mild chili pepper such as Poblano, minced
1/2 teaspoon freshly grated ginger
1 pound extra-lean ground beef
2 small ripe tomatoes, chopped
3 tablespoons fresh parsley, chopped
2 tablespoons chopped pimento-stuffed green olives
1 tablespoon vinegar
1/2 teaspoon thyme
1/4 teaspoon ground cinnamon
1/4 teaspoon ground allspice
1/4 teaspoon nutmeg
vegetable oil for frying

Sift together all dry ingredients for pastry into a bowl. With a pastry cutter or fork, cut in the shortening until mixture is crumbly. Continuing with the pastry cutter, add in the water until a stiff dough is formed. Cover with foil or plastic wrap and chill for 2 to 3 hours.

In a large deep skillet, heat the olive oil and sauté the onion until just clear. Add the garlic, chilies, and ginger and cook for an additional minute. Add the beef, breaking up the large chunks and cook thoroughly. In a colander, drain the excess fat.

Return beef to skillet and add the tomatoes and remaining ingredients except the oil for frying. Simmer gently over reduced heat for 10 minutes.

In the meantime remove the dough from the refrigerator and roll out on a floured board. Cut out large circles using an empty coffee can. Fill with 2 tablespoons of filling on one side and fold the other side over creating a half moon. Crimp edges with a fork.

Heat oil in a large deep skillet and fry the pates one at a time, turning over until golden. Drain on white paper towels. Serve at once.

Yield: 12 to 16 pates

> **Island Speak:** *Rock City*
> **Translation:** Local name for St. Thomas, U.S. Virgin Islands.

Cayman Pasties

Cayman Islands

Here is yet another version of these tasty meat tarts. The combination of apple, sour cream, and spices is just heavenly. I particularly like this recipe as it is considerably lower in calories than the preceding one, yet bursting with flavor.

Pastry:

See preceding recipe

Filling:

1 pound extra-lean ground beef
1/2 pound ground pork
1 small onion, minced
1 clove garlic, minced
1/2 cup heavy cream
1/2 teaspoon allspice
1/2 teaspoon cinnamon
1/4 teaspoon nutmeg
1/4 teaspoon cardamom
1 tablespoon habanero hot sauce
3/4 cup peeled, seeded and finely diced apple
2 tablespoons brown sugar
1 cup peeled and finely diced potato

2 egg yolks, beaten

Prepare the pastry as directed in the Virgin Island Beef Pate recipe and refrigerate for a couple of hours.

Sauté the beef, pork, garlic and onion. Drain in a colander and rinse with hot water to remove excess fat and calories.

Return to skillet adding cream, spices, and hot sauce. Simmer for about 10 minutes. Stir in brown sugar and fold in the apple and potato.

Preheat oven to 400°.

Remove dough from refrigerator and roll out on a floured surface, using a coffee can to cut out 5 inch rounds.

Place 2 heaping tablespoons of filling on one side of each round. Pinch edges together with a fork or pastry crimper.

Brush each side with egg yolk to form a lovely glaze. Place on an ungreased cookie sheet.

Bake at 400° until golden, approximately 12 to 15 minutes.

Serve at once.

Yield: about 24 pasties

Trinidadian Doubles
Trinidad

This East Indian version of Johnny Cakes goes nicely with curried chicken or vegetables. The uncooked doubles may also be frozen. Note, split pea flour can be found in East Indian groceries as well as readily available from the health food stores.

1 cup split pea flour
1/2 cup all-purpose flour
1 tablespoon sugar
1 tablespoon baking powder
1/2 teaspoon turmeric
1/2 teaspoon cumin
1/2 teaspoon salt
dash of nutmeg
1/4 cup water
vegetable oil for frying

Sift together the dry ingredients in a large bowl. Make a well in the center of the flour and gradually add in the water. Place a clean dish towel over the top of the bowl and set in a warm place for about 30 minutes. The dough will become puffy.

Heat the oil in a deep skillet. Form the dough into 2 to 3 inch flattened rounds and fry one at a time in the oil until golden. Drain on white paper towels.

Yield: approximately 24 depending upon size

Did you know? Plantains are part of the banana family and are 10 to 15 inches long with a much thicker skin than the banana. They are also much firmer, not as sweet and starchier which makes them ideal for cooking. Plantains like the banana, are high in potassium and a decent source of vitamin C, B6, magnesium and some vitamin A and folic acid.

Purchasing: The skin of plantains turns black when ripe. Choose firm ones, not soft and mushy.

Storing: Keep at room temperature unless extremely ripe, then refrigerate. Freeze by peeling first.

Preparation: Plantains may be baked in their skin. Wash thoroughly first and bake at 350° for approximately one hour. To grill, peel skin and make one inch thick diagonal slices and grill over medium heat for about 15 to 20 minutes on each side. Plantains may also be fried, peel and slice as for grilling. In a heated skillet, place a small pat of butter. Fry on each side until golden, draining on white paper towels.

Puerto Rican Plantain Tostones
Puerto Rico

While on a two week photo shoot in Puerto Rico, tostones were served as an accompaniment to nearly every meal. Plantains are in the banana family and the ones in this recipe call for unripe ones.

3 large green plantains
4 cups cold water
2 cloves garlic, minced
1 tablespoon sea salt
1/2 teaspoon sugar
vegetable oil for frying
salt and pepper to taste

Cut off the very tip of the plantain and peel like a banana. Slice diagonally about 1/2 inch thick.

Pour the water into a large bowl along with the garlic, salt and sugar. Soak the plantains for about 20 minutes. Drain on paper towels.

Fry in the hot oil for 2 to 3 minutes. Drain on white paper towels. Folding the towel over the slices, flatten with your hands. Quickly dip in salted water again and return to hot oil.

Fry until golden and drain once more on paper towels. Season with salt and pepper.

Yield: 24 to 30 tostones

Down Island Chewy Cornbread

St. Kitts

*A*lso called batter bread, this recipe was influenced by the African slaves that worked the sugar plantations who used their portion of bacon grease to tasty advantage.

1 1/2 cups self-rising yellow cornmeal
1/2 cup self-rising white flour
1/2 teaspoon baking powder
1/2 teaspoon salt
3 tablespoons sugar
1 cup buttermilk
2 eggs, beaten
2 tablespoons bacon grease
2 tablespoons minced jalapeno peppers
1 cup canned corn kernels, drained
1/4 cup boiling water

Preheat oven to 350°.

In a large bowl, stir together the cornmeal, flour, baking powder, salt and sugar. Stir in the buttermilk and eggs. Fold in the bacon grease along with the corn and jalapeno peppers. Mix in the water.

Pour into a hot greased iron skillet or oven-proof pan. Allow to sit 5 minutes as batter will puff slightly.

Bake at 350° for 15 to 20 minutes until just browned.

Yield: 4 to 6 servings

San Juan Ricemeal and Cheese Buns

Puerto Rico

Amojabanas are a very nice accompaniment to a fish dish or soup first course. Rice meal or flour can be found at the health food store.

2 cups buttermilk
2 tablespoons butter
1 teaspoon salt
1/2 teaspoon sugar
2 cups rice flour
2 teaspoons baking powder
1/4 teaspoon cardamom
3 eggs beaten
1cup grated mild semi-soft white cheese such as Muenster
vegetable oil for frying
salt and pepper to taste

In a medium saucepan bring the buttermilk, butter, salt and sugar to a boil. Remove from heat.

Sift together the rice flour, baking powder and cardamom. Slowly add this to the buttermilk mixture. Stir in eggs, combining well.

Return to medium heat and cook stirring constantly. Mixture will begin to separate from sides of pan.

Remove from heat and fold in grated cheese. Deep fry spoonfuls in hot fat until golden. Remove and drain on white paper towels, seasoning with salt and pepper.

Yield: 4 to 6 servings

Coconut Cornmeal Pudding
The Virgin Islands

This rich pudding is firm enough to be sliced and put on the plate next to pigeon peas and rice, fried plantain and jerked pork or chicken. Nice foil to curries and hot habanero sauces.

4 eggs, beaten
1 cup evaporated milk
1/2 cup sugar
1/2 teaspoon salt
1/4 teaspoon nutmeg
1/2 teaspoon cinnamon
2 cups white or yellow cornmeal
1/2 cup flour
1 cup freshly grated coconut
3/4 cup hot water
1/2 cup raisins

Whisk the eggs and the milk together and pour into a medium saucepan. Simmer until thickened, adding sugar, salt, and spices. Remove from heat and pour into large bowl.

Preheat oven to 350∞. Stir in the cornmeal, coconut, flour, and raisons along with the water until well combined. Pour into a large greased glass baking dish and bake for approximately 30 minutes. Batter will begin to brown and pull slightly from sides of pan.

Remove from oven and allow cooling for 15 minutes. Cut into 2-inch squares.

Yield: 6 to 8 servings

Cuban Calabaza Bread
Florida

This is one of my favorite breads—I can almost make a meal of it alone. The heady combination of almonds and spices pervade the kitchen with a perfume complimentary to slow Sunday mornings. Calabaza is a type of pumpkin—butternut squash may be substituted with equal success.

2 cups cooked and mashed calabaza
1/4 pound of butter, melted
1 teaspoon almond extract
1/2 teaspoon vanilla extract
5 eggs, beaten
1/4 cup honey
3/4 cup milk
4 cups all purpose flour
1 1/2 cups granulated sugar
1 teaspoon baking soda
1 tablespoon baking powder
1 teaspoon salt
1/2 teaspoon cardamom
1/2 teaspoon nutmeg
1/2 teaspoon allspice
1 teaspoon cinnamon
1/2 cup chopped almonds

Preheat oven to 350∞. Grease two 9 x 5 x 3-inch loaf pans.

In a large heavy bowl, combine the pumpkin, butter, extracts, eggs, milk and honey. In another bowl sift together the flour, sugar, baking powder and soda, salt and spices. Stir in the almonds. Combine with the pumpkin, mixing well, stirring in nuts.

Divide equally between the two pans. Bake for about 45 minutes, until a toothpick inserted in the center comes out clean.

Yield: 2 loaves

Mexican Black Bean Masa Cakes

Mexico

These gorditas (fat tortillas) are the Mexican equivalent of Caribbean "Johnny Cakes"—fried dough. Serve with any good flavorful salsa. This recipe while simple, requires a tortilla press available at Hispanic groceries.

1 cup cooked black beans (freshly made or canned)
1 crushed clove garlic
2 cups masa (dried or reconstituted)
1 teaspoon salt
vegetable oil for frying
pepper to taste
crumbled feta cheese or Mexican queso anejo
salsa

Process the beans and garlic in a food processor until smooth. Fold in the masa and salt. The dough should resemble cookie dough and not be too sticky. Divide and roll into balls the size of golf balls.

In a large skillet heat 1 inch of oil to about 375∞. Taking one of the dough balls, press until approximately 1/2 inch thick into a round. Slip the cake into the hot oil and turn quickly. Remove and drain on paper towels.

Serve while hot with salsa and crumbled cheese.

Yield: about 24 masa cakes

Island Speak: *I was badlucky today.*
Translation: I was unlucky today.

Arepas
Miami

This delicious corn and cheese pancake is a direct result of Miami's ever-growing Columbian population. The flour used here can be found in Hispanic markets and is made from cooked ground corn.

1 1/4 cups arepa flour
3/4 cup queso blanco or mild semi-soft white cheese
4 tablespoons melted butter
dash of cardamom
1 cup plus 2 tablespoons hot water
vegetable oil for frying
salt and pepper to taste

In a large bowl, combine the flour, cheese, cardamom, and butter. Gradually add in the water kneading to make a thick dough.

Form into balls and flatten with your hands to make 2 to 3 inch rounds about 1/2 inch in size.

Heat the vegetable oil in a 9-skillet and fry until golden. Drain on paper towels and season to taste.

Yield: 8 to 12 arepas

Antillean Shrimp Pastechis

Curacao

This puffy little pastry boasts an assortment of fillings from spicy meat to fish. Ideal finger food for cocktail parties.

Pastry:

6 cups all-purpose flour
2 teaspoons salt
4 tablespoons butter
2 tablespoons shortening
2 eggs, beaten
1 1/2 cups water

filling:
2 tablespoons vegetable oil
1/4 cup minced onion
1/2 teaspoon chili powder
1/4 cup chopped stewed tomato from can
1 pound cooked shrimp, shelled, deveined and chopped
dash of habanero hot sauce
1/4 cup breadcrumbs
1 egg, beaten
vegetable oil for frying

Sift the flour and the salt into a large bowl. With a pastry cutter, cut in the butter and shortening. Gradually add the water and beaten eggs, making a pliable dough—kneading until smooth. On a well-floured surface, roll out the dough and use a small empty coffee can to cut out circles (around 3 to 4 inches in diameter)

In a large skillet, sauté the onion in the oil until clear. Add the chili powder, tomato, shrimp, and hot sauce. Fold in breadcrumbs and remove from heat.

Place 2 tablespoons of filling in center of each circle and fold over pinching edges together. Brush with beaten egg.

In a large skillet filled with at least 1 inch of heated oil, fry until golden. Drain on paper towels.

Yield: 3 to 4 dozen pastechis

Coconut Cornmeal Rings
Dominican Republic

Rosqueticos are a rich baked corn bread with a hard texture. These will keep in tightly sealed container in a cool pantry for up to a week.

3 cups yellow cornmeal
1 cup cornstarch
1 teaspoon salt
2 tablespoons sugar
1 teaspoon baking powder
1/4 teaspoon cinnamon
1/4 teaspoon nutmeg
3/4 cup vegetable shortening
1/4 butter
3 eggs, beaten
1 cup unsweetened coconut milk
granulated sugar to dust

Preheat oven to 375∞. Grease a cookie sheet generously.

Sift together the cornmeal, cornstarch, sugar, baking powder, spices and salt. With a fork cut in the shortening and butter. In a separate bowl, whisk together the eggs and coconut milk. Gradually stir into the flour to make a firm dough. Allow to sit for 10 minutes.

On a floured surface roll out the dough to make a long roll about 1 inch in diameter. Cut into 3 to 4 inch strips and pinch ends together to make a circle.

Arrange circles on cookie sheet and bake for 25 to 30 minutes.

Remove and cool on rack, dusting lightly with granulated sugar while still hot.

Yield: approximately 2 dozen

Island Dumplins
Grenada

Dumplings are readily found in all sorts and soups and stews all over the Caribbean. I particularly like this recipe that I found in a pretty open-air restaurant surrounded by palms and lush tropical flowers.

2 cups all-purpose flour
1/2 teaspoon salt
1 tablespoon baking powder
1/4 teaspoon nutmeg
1/4 teaspoon cinnamon
1/4 teaspoon allspice
1/4 teaspoon cardamom
2 tablespoons butter
cold water

Sift all dry ingredients into a large heavy bowl. Using a fork, cut in the butter until crumbly. Add cold water by the tablespoon until the dough has a firm consistency, like play-dough.

Knead until smooth and form into ping-pong size balls. The dumplings may be directly cooked along with the soup or stew during the last 10 minutes or dropped into boiling salted water.

Yield: 18 to 24 dumplings

Mexican Macaroni and Cheese
Mexico

Nearly every holiday gathering I have attended in St. Thomas at a West Indian home has served macaroni and cheese. My husband's grandmother Anna indeed served one of the best. When it was my turn to bring a dish, I surprised everyone by this version I picked up while in Cancun. Fortunately, West Indians are fond of anything hot, so this spicy version went over well.

1/3 cup all-purpose flour
8 ounces condensed milk
1/2 cup shredded extra-sharp Cheddar cheese
1/2 cup grated Parmesan cheese
1/2 cup shredded Muenster cheese
1 2/3 cups 2% milk
6 cups cooked elbow macaroni
2 tablespoons chopped jalapeno peppers
1/2 roasted red pepper, minced
cayenne pepper to taste
butter
Preheat oven to 375∞. Butter a 2-quart glass baking dish and set aside.

In a medium saucepan place flour. Slowly whisk in the condensed milk and cheeses, stirring until smooth and no lumps remain. Cook over low heat until milk is hot. Keep stirring until melted. Do not let the mixture bubble as this will separate and ruin the cheese. Add in 2% milk and keep stirring.

Remove from heat, stir in macaroni, roasted and jalapeno peppers. Season with cayenne.

Pour into buttered dish.

Bake until slightly browned on top.

Starfruit Nutted Rice with Raisons

St. Eustatius

Staysha is a tiny 12-mile square island in the Netherlands Antilles.

2 tablespoons water
2 tablespoons granulated sugar
1 large starfruit or carambola, minced
1 tablespoon olive oil
1 small onion, minced
1 teaspoon chicken bouillon granules
1/2 teaspoon ground cinnamon
1/2 teaspoon ground allspice
2 cups hot cooked basmati rice
1/2 cup toasted crushed cashews
1/2 cup golden raisins

salt and pepper to taste

In a small saucepan, heat the water and stir in the granulated sugar until melted. Add in the starfruit and bring to a simmer for 5 minutes. Remove from heat and set aside.

Heat the olive oil in a medium saucepan and cook the onion until just clear. Add in chicken bouillon, and spices, stirring and cooking for 1 minute. Stir in the starfruit mixture, gently fold in the rice coating evenly. Add nuts, raisins and combine with hot rice.

Serve at once.

Yield: 4 servings

Festival Rice

British Virgin Islands

The British Virgin Islands are a short ferry ride from the U.S. Virgin islands, but worlds apart. Life is quiet and laid back.

1 cup long-grain white rice
1 1/2 cups hot chicken broth
1/2 teaspoon turmeric
1/2 teaspoon cumin
1 tablespoon olive oil, divided
1 small yellow onion, minced
1 clove garlic, crushed
1/2 small red bell pepper, chopped
1/2 small green bell pepper, chopped
1/2 cup canned pigeon peas or black-eyed peas, drained
3 tablespoons fresh chopped parsley
juice of 1 lemon
1/2 teaspoon lemon zest

Combine the rice and broth in a medium saucepan. Add 1 teaspoon olive oil, bring to a boil, reduce heat, and cook for about 20 minutes until water is absorbed.

In a small sauté pan, heat the spices until lightly toasted and aroma released. Add the remaining oil and sauté the onions, garlic, and peppers. Stir in the black-eyed peas.

Fold the onion mixture into the rice carefully and evenly. Add parsley, lemon juice and zest—turn and mix.

Goes well with any fruit or coconut based main dish.

Yield: 4 servings

Festival Rice Stuffed Green Peppers
British Virgin Islands

Easy to prepare ahead and freeze for tasty emergency dinners.

4 medium uniform green bell peppers
2 cups cooked Festival Rice
2 cups tomato juice
1 cup shredded sharp cheddar cheese
paprika

Preheat oven to 350∞.

Cut peppers in half lengthwise and remove fiber and seeds.

Spoon the Festival Rice evenly into pepper shells. Sprinkle with cheddar cheese and top with dash of paprika.

Pour tomato juice into 13 x 9-inch baking dish. Place filled peppers in sauce. Cover with aluminum foil being careful to leave a little space so that the cheese does not stick and bake for 20 minutes.

Spoon tomato juice over peppers and serve.

Yield: 8 servings

Island
Seafoods

Seafood is as indigenous to the Caribbean as palm trees and beaches. The islanders made liberal use of the ocean's bounty and complimented it with the riches of the land. Try the interesting Citrus Sauce, Creole Sauce, Jerked Fish or the fancy variation on the old standby Coconut Shrimp, Cointreau-Rum Coconut Shrimp. Seafood is a delicious and healthy alternative to red meat or chicken.

Sweet and Spicy Crusted Swordfish with Citrus Sauce

Grenada

Cinnamon, ginger and pistachios make for a heavenly crust on this fish.

1/4 cup crushed pistachios
2 tablespoons seasoned Italian breadcrumbs
1 teaspoon freshly ground ginger
1/2 teaspoon ground cinnamon
1 tablespoon brown sugar
1/4 teaspoon salt
1/2 teaspoon freshly ground black pepper
4 (8-ounce) swordfish steaks, about 1/2 inch thick
2 teaspoons olive oil
1/2 teaspoon fresh lemon zest
2 tablespoons fresh lemon juice
2 tablespoons frozen orange juice concentrate
1/4 cup fresh grapefruit sections finely diced
1 tablespoon honey

In a small bowl, combine the nuts, breadcrumbs, ginger, cinnamon, brown sugar, salt and pepper. Coat both sides of the swordfish with this.

Heat 1 teaspoon of the oil in a large non-stick skillet over medium heat. Sauté fish 5 to 6 minutes on each side. Test for doneness when fish flakes with a fork.

In a small saucepan, combine the remaining 1 teaspoon of oil, lemon zest, juices, grapefruit sections and honey. Bring to boil and quickly reduce heat, remove from stove.

To serve, drizzle sauce over the fish.

Yield: 4 servings

Deserted Island Tuna with Pineapple Mayonnaise

Antigua

This beautiful island with a beach for every day of the year and over 143 species of birds was the setting for Speed II and episodes of The Young and Restless.

4 (8-ounce) tuna steaks, about 1-inch thick
1/2 cup mayonnaise
1/2 cup low-fat plain yogurt
2 tablespoons Pineapple Hazelnut Chutney
1 teaspoon fresh chopped tarragon
1/2 teaspoon fresh zest of lemon
1 tablespoon olive oil

Preheat gas or charcoal grill.

In a small bowl, combine the mayonnaise, yogurt, chutney, tarragon and lemon. Set aside.

Brush the grill with the olive oil. Place tuna on grill topping with 1 teaspoon of the mayonnaise. Cook until desired doneness.

Serve with Pineapple Mayonaise.

Yield: 4 servings

Island Speak: I ain't in this wid allyuh.
Translation: You're on your own here; I'm not involved in your scam.

Reggae Pasta with Lobster and Almond Pesto

Anguilla

Anguilla is celebrated for its spiny Caribbean lobster—similar to our Maine lobster, but not as rich—snapper and grouper.

1/4 cup chopped almonds
1 cup fresh chopped parsley
2 tablespoons olive oil
1 clove garlic, crushed
1 tablespoon lemon juice
1/2 teaspoon lemon zest
1/4 teaspoon cumin
1/2 teaspoon salt
1/4 teaspoon coriander
1 tablespoon olive oil
1/2 cup chopped yellow onion
1/2 cup chopped green bell pepper
1/2 cup chopped red bell pepper
1 tablespoon butter
1 pound cooked lobster meat
1 tablespoon white wine
2 cups hot cooked angel-hair pasta
freshly ground pepper to taste

In a food processor, puree the almonds, parsley, 2 tablespoons olive oil, garlic, lemon juice, zest, cumin, salt and coriander until smooth.

In a medium skillet heat the 1 tablespoon olive oil and sauté the onion until clear, along with the peppers. Remove vegetables from skillet and set aside.

Melt the butter in the same saucepan along with the wine over medium high heat. Add the lobster, torn in bite-size pieces and reheat gently for 2 to 3 minutes over low heat.. Do not over cook. Add vegetables back to skillet with the wine, removing immediately from heat.

Toss the pesto with the pasta, carefully fold in the lobster meat.

Divide between 2 plates and season with ground pepper.

Yield: 2 servings

Island Speak: *Wha good fo da liber is bad fo da spleen.*
Translation: What's good for one person, is bad for the other.

Creole Red Snapper

St. Martin

What do you do while in St. Martin? Why go to the beach and eat of course! Even serious diners can dine at a different restaurant each night of a two-week stay. Serve with fungi and fried plantains.

2 lbs. fillet of red snapper
juice of 3 limes
1 small onion, minced
1 clove garlic, minced
dash of grated ginger
3 tablespoons butter
all purpose flour
1 red bell pepper, slivered
1 green bell pepper, slivered
2 cloves garlic, minced
1 medium yellow onion, minced
2 large ripe tomatoes, peeled and diced
1/4 cup sundried tomatoes, soaked in hot water
1 tablespoon tomato paste
salt and pepper to taste

In a shallow glass dish, combine the lime juice, small onion, garlic clove and ginger. Marinate the fish, cut in portions in the refrigerator for a couple of hours.

Heat the butter in a heavy skillet while dredging the fillets in flour. Fry over hot fire until lightly browned and crisp—drain on white paper towels—keeping warm in oven.

In the same skillet, sauté the peppers, two garlic cloves and onion. Add the tomatoes, simmering for approximately 15 to 20 minutes until the sauce is thick. Adjust taste with salt. Return the fillets to the skillet and coat gently with the sauce and heat through.

Yield: 4 servings

Kingston Jerked Fish

Jamaica, mon

Fish is one of the easiest and quickest ways to enjoy jerk. Look for a firm fish with few bones that does not fall apart easily when cooked.

6 8-ounce swordfish, kingfish or other firm fish steaks
juice of 2 lemons and 1 limes
1 teaspoon ground allspice
1/2 teaspoon cinnamon
1/2 teaspoon nutmeg
1/2 teaspoon thyme
1/2 cup scallion, finely chopped
4 scotch bonnet peppers, seeded and minced
2 tablespoons cider vinegar
3 tablespoons soy sauce
2 tablespoon vegetable oil
1 tablespoon salt

Put all ingredients in blender except fish steaks. Place the steaks in a shallow glass dish and pour marinade over—turning to coat. Chill in refrigerator at least one hour.

Over hot grill, cook steaks 5 to 7 minutes on each side, continuously basting with remaining marinade.

Serve with ice-cold beer.

Yield: 6 servings

Island Speak: *Everyting kopasetic*
Translation: Everything is absolutely perfect, fantastic.

Antillean Barbequed Tuna
with Fresh Mango-Tomato Salsa
Aruba

*A*ruba's restaurants serve an international variety of cuisines. This hot and cool combination is terrific with the exotic taste of coconut and ginger in the fruity salsa.

6 8-ounce tuna steaks
1/3 cup fresh lime juice
1/4 cup cream of coconut
1 tablespoon freshly grated ginger.

salsa:
2 teaspoons honey
2 tablespoons lime juice
1 tablespoon rum
1 large ripe tomato, diced
1 ripe mango, peeled and diced
1 small cucumber, peeled and diced
1/4 cup fresh cilantro, finely chopped
3 green onions, minced
1/2 small scotch bonnet pepper, seeded and minced

Marinate the tuna in the 1/3 cup fresh lime juice, cream of coconut and ginger using a shallow baking dish. Place in refrigerator for a couple of hours.

Prepare salsa by stirring together honey, lime juice and rum. Pour over other ingredients evenly and toss gently. Allow to sit at room temperature while fish is marinating.

Grill tuna over hot barbeque for 5 minutes per side until degree of doneness is desired—basting with lime-coconut marinade.

Turn onto plates and spoon salsa over the top. Serve with rice and green salad.

Yield: 6 servings

Savory Crab Stew
Guadeloupe

Similar to Tobago's Crab Pilau, this dish is locally known as matoutou. For Crab Pilau, use coconut milk instead of water.

1/4 cup olive oil
6 garlic cloves
1 small yellow onion, minced
2 pounds crab meat, carefully picked over
1/2 teaspoon fresh chopped thyme
1/4 teaspoon cumin
3 tablespoons lime juice
1/2 teaspoon fresh lime zest
1/2 habanero pepper, seeded and minced
1 cube chicken bouillon
4 cups water
2 cups white rice

In a large deep saucepan, heat the oil and sauté the onion and garlic for 2 minutes. Add the crab and cook over low heat for another 2 minutes. Add remaining ingredients except rice and simmer for 3 minutes.

Add water and bring to a boil; reduce heat. Add rice, cooking until the water is absorbed and rice tender—about 25 to 35 minutes.

Season with additional salt and pepper if necessary.

Yield: 6 servings

Peppery Conch Salad

Bahamas

This is definitely one of the Bahamas more popular dishes. Adjust the fire up or down by reducing the amount of pepper added. The mango balances the chewy conch and heat of the pepper.

1 pound conch, cleaned, pounded and coarsely run through a food processor
2/3 cup fresh lime juice
1 small habanero pepper, seeded and minced
1 small red onion, minced
1/2 cucumber, chopped
2 tablespoons celery, minced
1 tablespoon olive oil
salt and pepper to taste
3/4 cup fresh mango, diced

In a large bowl, combine all ingredients except the mango. Marinate overnight in the refrigerator.

The next morning gently fold in the mango and refrigerate until thoroughly chilled.

Serve with mixed greens and hard-boiled eggs.

Yield: 6 servings

Shrimp with Creole Barbeque Sauce

St. Martin

Here is another good Creole recipe from French St. Martin. The barbeque sauce can be used with equal success on meat, pork or chicken.

2 lbs. large shrimp peeled and deveined

sauce:

1 tablespoon vegetable oil
1 medium onion, minced
1/2 cup dry red wine
2 tablespoons red wine vinegar
1 tablespoon tomato paste
1/4 cup freshly pureed mango
3 tablespoons tamarind paste
1 clove garlic, minced
2 tablespoons dark brown sugar
1/2 teaspoon chili powder
1/2 teaspoon ground cumin
1/4 teaspoon curry powder
1/2 teaspoon salt

Sauté the onion in the vegetable oil until just clear. Add remaining ingredients except shrimp, bring to boil, reduce heat and simmer for 10 minutes. Remove from heat.

Place shrimp in shallow dish, pour marinade over the top and refrigerate for a couple of hours.

Place shrimp on skewers and grill over hot fire for about 5 minutes, basting constantly.

Serve hot with rice and fried plantains.

Yield: 4 servings

Salmon with Brown Sugar and Lime Rum-Mustard Glaze
Tortola, British Virgin Islands

The nice thing with this recipe is that you can wrap the fish in foil and walk away from the fire without worrying about turning the fish or any sticking to grill.

glaze:
1 tablespoon brown sugar
1 tablespoon honey
1 tablespoon butter
2 tablespoons spicy mustard, Dijon-style
1 teaspoon freshly grated ginger
1/2 teaspoon freshly grated lime zest
1 tablespoon rum
1 tablespoon olive oil
1/2 teaspoon salt
pepper to taste

4 8-ounce salmon fillets

Sauté the brown sugar in the honey and butter until melted and thickened slightly. Remove from heat and stir in remaining ingredients besides fish.

Place the salmon skin side down on the four individual sheets of foil, pouring the marinade over the top. Fold over foil and seal. Grill over medium heat for about 20 minutes.

Remove from heat and use a spatula to separate the skin from the fillet. Serve at once.

Yield: 4 servings

> **Island Speak: *Manana***
> **Translation:** A favorite island expression and way of life, meaning whenever we get to it, which is unknown.

Jamaican Salt Fish and Ackee

Jamaica

This third-largest island in the Caribbean (after Cuba and Puerto Rico) offers an abundance of physical attractions such as endless beaches, rushing waterfalls and jungle-topped mountains. This is Jamaica's national dish highlighting the ackee fruit whose meat is quite similar to scrambled eggs. Ackees may only be consumed when the fruit is completely ripe—when the pod has become red and is split open, displaying the black seeds and yellow flesh. Unripe ackee is poisonous. Canned ackee may be found in Jamaican groceries

1 pound salt cod
1-pound 2-ounce can ackees or 24 fresh ackees
3 tablespoons vegetable oil
1 onion, minced
1 tomato, diced
1/2 small scotch bonnet pepper, seeded, and minced
3 slices crisp bacon, crumbled
salt and pepper to taste

Soak the salt cod in water, overnight in the refrigerator to remove the excess salt. Drain the water and rinse. Boil the cod in a large pot filled with water for 15 minutes. Remove with a slotted spoon and set aside to cool. When cool, flake the fish with a fork.

To clean the ackee, remove the black seeds and the pink membrane. Boil the ackee for 5 minutes and remove from hot water, setting aside.

In a large deep skillet, heat the oil, sauté the onion and tomato until the onion is clear. Add the ackee, cod, hot peppers, adding salt and pepper to taste. Gently stir to refrain from breaking up the ackee and cook for 5 to 6 minutes. At the last minute, toss in the bacon to keep it crisp.

Yield: 4 to 6 servings.

Ponce Oven-Fried Fish with Mojo Sauce
Puerto Rico

Any whole fish can be used in this recipe. The fish is liberally coated and stuffed with fragrant spices (adobo paste) and baked in the oven until the skin is crisp. Lovely with the local Mojo Sauce and Puerto Rican Black Beans and Rice. A mortar and pestle is needed for this recipe, one of the traditional utensils integral to authentic Puerto Rican cuisine.

10 to 12 cloves of garlic, peeled
1/2 small onion, minced
2 teaspoons cracked black pepper corns
1 tablespoon fresh oregano, chopped
3 teaspoons sea salt
1/2 teaspoon cumin
1/2 cup olive oil

4 whole fish of choice, 1 to 2 pounds, cleaned with head left on

Place the garlic, onion, peppercorns, and salt in the mortar. Use an up and down motion with the pestle to break up the ingredients. Add the fresh oregano and cumin and continue pounding. Slowly add in the olive oil to make a smooth paste and set aside.

Rinse fish, dry and place on cutting board. Make diagonal slits on both sides of the belly of the fish and place on a baking sheet. Stuff the slits with the adobo paste and liberally coat the outside of the fish. Marinate in the refrigerator for at least 2 hours.

Preheat the oven to 350∞. Bake for 20 minutes until the skin is crisp. The flesh should be flaky.

Mojo Sauce:

1/2 cup olive oil
1 medium yellow onion, minced
1 small scotch bonnet, peeled, and seeded
6 garlic cloves, peeled, and minced
1 cup tomato sauce
1/3 alcaparrado or chopped Manzanilla olives
1/2 red bell pepper, roasted, peeled and finely chopped

1 large ripe tomato
1 tablespoon fresh oregano
1/4 cup fresh culantro (wide coriander leaf available in Hispanic groceries) or fresh cilantro may be substituted

In a large heavy skillet, sauté the onion, garlic and scotch bonnet pepper in the olive oil until the onion is just clear.

Add the tomato sauce, olives, roasted bell pepper, tomato, and fresh oregano and bring to a boil, reducing to a simmer. Simmer for 3 minutes and remove from heat, stirring in chopped culantro or cilantro.

Serve over the hot fish with beans and rice.

Yield: 4 servings

Santo Domingo Marinated Fish
Dominican Republic

Santo Domingo, the capitol, is the oldest inhabited city in the Western Hemisphere. Columbus landed on the island in 1492 and wrecked his ship, the Santa Maria on December 24.

4 to 6 fillets of firm white fish
2 tablespoons fresh lemon juice
1 cup all-purpose flour
1/4 cup olive oil
1/4 cup fresh lime juice
1 tablespoon orange juice concentrate
1/2 teaspoon freshly grated lime zest
1/2 teaspoon orange zest
dash of cinnamon
5 garlic cloves, peeled, and minced
2 scallions, finely chopped
1 large yellow onion, minced
3 tablespoons pimento-stuffed olives
2 teaspoons capers
1 teaspoon tomato paste
1/2 teaspoon cumin
2 limes

Squeeze the lemon juice over the fish fillets and dredge in the flour. In a heavy skillet, heat the olive oil and fry the fish over medium heat until lightly browned on both sides. Place the fish in a glass dish.

In a small bowl, combine the fresh lime juice, orange juice concentrate, lime and orange zest, cinnamon, garlic, scallion, yellow onion, olives, capers, tomato paste and cumin until smoothly blended.

Pour this over the fish and refrigerate overnight. Serve chilled with lime wedges.

Yield: 4 to 6 servings

Havana Almond Fish

Cuba

Cuban cuisine is rapidly becoming the rage in the United States, particularly in the Miami region. Any firm white fish will do well.

3/4 cup crushed almonds
4 garlic cloves, peeled
1 medium yellow onion, peeled and chopped
1 teaspoon freshly ground black pepper
1 tablespoon fresh cilantro
1 teaspoon powdered cumin
1 teaspoon granulated sugar
juice of one lemon
grating of lemon zest
dash of coriander
1 tablespoon dry port wine
2 tablespoons olive oil
6 firm white fish fillets, about 6 to 8 ounces
salt to taste

In a food processor or using a mortar and pestle, grind the almonds, garlic, onion, black pepper, cilantro, cumin, sugar, lemon juice and zest, coriander and port wine to a paste.

Coat the fish fillets evenly on all sides with the almond paste. Refrigerate until thoroughly chilled.

Heat the olive oil in a large, heavy skillet sauté the fish until both sides are lightly browned and flakes easily using a fork. Salt to taste.

Serve with hot white rice and a green salad.

Yield: 6 servings

Swordfish with Walnut Malanga Crust
Miami

This Cuban recipe consists of coating fish fillets with a crust of root vegetables. Malanga is a tuber similar to yam, but sweeter and nuttier in taste. Yam or yucca may be substituted in this recipe.

3 pounds of malanga or yam, peeled and grated
1 beaten egg
1/2 cup cornmeal
1/2 pound ground walnuts
4 (6 to 8 ounce) swordfish fillets
oil for frying
salt and pepper to taste

In a large bowl, combine the malanga, beaten egg, cornmeal and ground walnuts.

Rinse and dry the fish fillets, seasoning with salt and pepper. Firmly encase each fillet with a thick coating of the malanga, about 1/4 inch thick.

In a deep skillet, heat about 1/2 inch of oil. Carefully place 1 to 2 fillets into skillet using a wide spatula. Fry until golden, about 2 minutes per side. Use care when turning so that the crust does not break off.

Drain on clean white paper towels. Serve with rice, beans and a crisp garden salad.

Yield: 4 servings

Bahamian Coconut Fish Fingers
Bahamas

This delightful variation of coconut shrimp is excellent with cold beer. The crème of coconut can be found in the gourmet section of your grocery store.

3 eggs beaten
3 tablespoons crème of coconut
3 tablespoons milk
3 tablespoons all-purpose flour
1/2 teaspoon baking powder
2 pounds grouper or red snapper fillet, cut into inch-wide strips
3/4 cup grated, unsweetened coconut
oil for frying
salt and pepper to taste

In a small bowl, combine the beaten eggs, crème of coconut, milk, flour and baking powder. Roll the fish in the batter and dip into the grated coconut.

Heat the oil in a deep skillet. Fry fish sticks on all sides until golden. Do not over cook. Drain on white paper towels. Season with salt and pepper.

Crab and Coconut Pastelillos

Puerto Rico

Pastelillos are tiny turnovers, which can be filled with chicken, ham, meat, sausage or shellfish. These turnovers are part of an assortment of fried finger foods ever popular in Puerto Rico. The following recipe may be deep fried, but I prefer a lighter, baked version.

1/4 cup olive oil
2 garlic cloves, crushed
1 teaspoon freshly grated ginger
1 small yellow onion, minced
1 small jalapeno pepper, minced
1 1/4 pounds fresh crab meat, carefully picked over
1/2 cup coconut milk
1/4 cup condensed milk
1 tablespoon lime juice
1/2 teaspoon fresh lime zest
1 tablespoon chopped fresh cilantro
1 teaspoon fresh oregano
1/2 teaspoon cumin
1 small red bell pepper, chopped
6 small green, pimento-stuffed olives, chopped

pastry:
1 cup warm water
1 tablespoon brown sugar
1 cup active yeast
3 cups all-purpose flour
1 teaspoon salt

1 stick butter, chilled
1 egg, beaten

In a skillet, sauté the garlic, ginger, onion and jalapeno pepper for 2 minutes in the 1/2 cup oil. Add the crab, coconut milk and condensed milk cooking over low heat for 5 minutes. Add remaining ingredients, simmer for 2 more minutes and then remove from heat.

To make the pastry: combine the warm water, sugar, yeast in a cup, and let sit for several minutes.

In a large bowl, combine the flour and salt. Use a fork or pastry cutter to cut the butter into the flour until crumbly. Making a well in the center, pour in the water and yeast. Knead together for 6 or 7 minutes. Cover the bowl and allow to rise for an hour.

Punch down dough and knead for several more minutes. Cut dough in half and make a long roll. Divide this roll into six pieces and cover. Allow to rise an additional 45 minutes.

On a well-floured surface, roll each ball flat, until approximately 6 inches in diameter.

Preheat oven to 375∞.

Place 3 tablespoons of crab filling in center and pinch edges shut with fingers. Make impressions around the edges with a fork. Brush with beaten egg to impart a glossy sheen to the pastelillos. Bake until golden about 10 to 12 minutes.

Yield: 12 pastelillos

Did you know? Carpet, rope, baskets, and fabric are made from leaves of the coconut tree. Coconut palms, which grow in all tropical climates can attain as much as 100 feet in height. The fruits grow in clusters of 5 or 6 and I have seen them fall from trees like bombs. The fruit is encased in a green pericap. On the inside is the familiar hairy brown shell, white meat on the inside and a whitish liquid, which is very good. In the islands immature coconuts are harvested, chilled, tops cut off with a machete and the refreshing liquid drank directly from the shell. Good source of potassium, copper, iron, magnesium, zinc, phosphorous and folic acid.

Purchasing: Select uncracked coconuts that are full of liquid. Be sure that the eyes are solid and contain no mold.

Storing: Whole coconuts will keep for several months in a cool spot. Keep opened coconuts covered with water in the refrigerator for a week.

Preparation: Punch holes through the eyes and drain the milk, reserve. Crack the shell by putting on solid floor and hitting with a hammer.

Star Shrimp Pasta

St. John, U.S. Virgin Islands

A lovely restaurant overlooking Cruz Bay harbor produced this recipe quite a few years ago. Before it changed hands, the owner generously shared the recipe with me. Quick and simple to make, star fruit or carambola add a pretty touch.

3 tablespoons olive oil
2 garlic cloves, crushed
1 medium yellow onion, minced
1/2 small habanero pepper, minced
1 large firm tomatoes, peeled and diced
1 1/4 pounds of cleaned and shelled shrimp
2 tablespoons dry sherry
2 cups water
2 cups chicken broth
1 12-ounce package fettuccine noodles
2 ripe star fruit (medium yellow, no green)

freshly ground black pepper

In a deep skillet, sauté the garlic, onion, pepper and tomato for 1 1/2 minutes in the olive oil. Add the shrimp and sherry and cook until just pink. Set aside in warm oven.

Bring water and chicken broth to boil. Cook noodles in this broth until al dente. Drain.

Toss in the shrimp and star fruit mixture, stirring gently and heating through. Serve at once.

Yield: 4 servings

Poisson en Blaff

Martinique

This lively poached fish dish is very popular in the French islands of Guadeloupe and Martinique. Theory has it that the fish makes the "blaff" sound when it hits the poaching liquid.

3 cups of water
4 tablespoons lime juice
3 tablespoons lemon juice
1/2 teaspoon lemon zest
3 garlic cloves, crushed
1 hot chili pepper, seeded and minced
2 teaspoons salt
1 cup dry white wine
2 medium scallions, thinly sliced
2 whole cloves
1/2 teaspoon allspice berries
1 bay leaf
2 (1-pound) red snappers, cleaned, scaled with heads and tails left on
freshly ground pepper to taste

In a deep dish, combine 2 cups water, 4 tablespoons lime and lemon juice, lemon zest, 2 garlic cloves, hot pepper and salt. Place fish in dish and marinate in refrigerator for 1 hour.

Remove fish from marinade and discard marinade.. In a large skillet, combine 1 cup water, wine, garlic clove and all other ingredients except the fish. Simmer over low heat for 6 minutes. Add the fish and simmer for another 10 to 12 minutes. Season with pepper.

Serve with white rice and yams.

Yield: 2 servings

Shrimp Colombo
Guadeloupe

Colombo is similar to curry and indigenous to the French Caribbean Islands.

2 pounds cleaned and shelled shrimp
4 cups water
1/2 cup dry white wine
2 tablespoons curry powder
4 tablespoons peanut oil
1 large yellow onion, minced
2 cloves garlic, crushed
1 small hot chili pepper, seeded and minced
1 tablespoons flour
1/2 cup coconut milk
1 cup chicken broth
juice of two limes
1 tablespoon tamarind pump or Mango Chutney
2 tablespoons dry Madeira
1 tablespoon freshly ground pepper
cooked hot white rice

Poach the shrimp in the water and wine, until barely pink. Discard the liquid and reserve the shrimp.

In a large dry skillet, gently toast the curry powder until slightly darkened in color and an aromatic fragrance is released. Add the oil and sauté the onion, garlic and pepper. Stir in the flour, and slowly pour in the chicken broth and coconut milk, stirring constantly. Add all remaining ingredients except rice and cook for another 3 minutes.

Serve over the white rice.

Yield: 4 servings

Run Down

Jamaica

The sweet custard in this dish is produced when the water boils out of the coconut milk and "runs down" into a custard.

1 1/2 pounds pickled mackerel fillet or herring, cut in 2-inch slices
2 cups coconut milk
1 medium yellow onion, minced
1/2 teaspoon lemon zest
1 habanero pepper, seeded and minced
2 cloves garlic, crushed
1 teaspoon malt vinegar
1/2 teaspoon fresh thyme
1 large ripe tomato, peeled and diced
chopped chives

Immerse the fish in cold water for at least one hour. Rinse and set aside.

Boil the coconut milk for 15 minutes. Add all remaining ingredients except chives and simmer for 20 minutes. Garnish with chives and serve with boiled green bananas.

Yield: 2 servings

Cointreau-rum Coconut shrimp
The Bahamas

Each island has its own recipe for coconut shrimp. I particularly enjoyed this one as it uses graham cracker crumbs instead of just flour alone.

1 cup crushed graham cracker crumbs
1 cup all-purpose flour
4 eggs, beaten
1 cup unsweetened coconut milk
1 tablespoon Cointreau
1 tablespoon rum
2 pounds jumbo shrimp, peeled and deveined
2 cups unsweetened flaked coconut (fresh if possible)
oil for frying

In a medium bowl, combine the cracker crumbs, flour, eggs, coconut milk, Cointreau and rum..

Dip the shrimp in the batter then dredge in the coconut flakes. Deep fry until golden, do not burn. Drain on white paper towels.

Serve with chutney and a good hot sauce.

Yield: 4 servings

Meat Lover's Paradise

Pork Fajitas with Orange-Avocado Salsa
Cuba

Cuban is food is enjoying an ever-growing Renaissance not only in the Caribbean, but in the United States as well.

1 pound pork tenderloin
1 tablespoon olive oil
3 large garlic cloves, crushed
1 small yellow onion, sliced in strips
zest of one lime
1 green bell pepper, sliced in strips
1 cube chicken bullion
1 teaspoon chili powder
4 tablespoons hot water
8 (7-inch) flour tortillas
Orange-Avocado Salsa
sour cream

Preheat oven to 375∞.

Place pork on a broiler pan so that the fat drains away and bake for approximately 30 minutes. Use a meat thermometer and be sure the meat has attained a temperature of 160∞. Remove from oven and set aside.

In a medium skillet, heat the oil adding the garlic, onion, lime zest, and pepper. Stir the chicken bouillon and chili powder into the hot water. Add the onion mixture, cooking just until the onion turns clear. Remove from heat.

Bake tortillas according to package directions. While baking cut the pork in think slices about 2 to 3 inches long. Arrange the pork on each tortilla along with the vegetables. Spoon salsa over the pork, serving with sour cream.

Yield: 4 servings

Orange-Avocado Salsa

2 medium oranges, peeled, sections and chopped
1 large ripe avocado, peeled and diced
1 tablespoon Cointreau Mango Chutney
1/4 cup minced red onion
1/2 cup ripe tomato, diced
1/4 cup diced celery
1 garlic clove, crushed
1 tablespoon olive oil
2 tablespoons fresh lime juice
1/4 teaspoon salt
2 tablespoons chopped cilantro
freshly ground black pepper
1 tablespoon fiery hot sauce

Toss lightly all ingredients except the garlic, oil, lime juice, salt, pepper, hot sauce, and cilantro in a medium bowl.

In a small cup stir together remaining ingredients. Pour over the avocado mixture and mix carefully.

Yield: 2 cups

Island Speak: *Tek time walk fas'.*
Translation: In other words, what's the rush?

Curried Pork Chops with Tropical Fruit Salsa
Martinique

Pork makes a nice alternative to red meat or chicken.

2 tablespoons Cointreau Mango Chutney
1 tablespoon frozen orange juice concentrate
2 teaspoons curry powder
1 teaspoon freshly grated ginger
1/2 teaspoon ground cumin
1 teaspoon olive oil
4 (6-ounce) center-cut loin pork chops
salt and pepper to taste

Tropical Fruit Salsa:
2 tablespoons fresh lemon juice
1/2 teaspoon fresh lemon zest
1 tablespoon honey
1 tablespoon chopped fresh cilantro
1 tablespoon hot pepper sauce
1/4 teaspoon cumin
1/2 cup ripe, but firm papaya chunks
1/2 cup fresh diced pineapple
1/2 cup diced pink grapefruit sections
1/2 cup chopped seedless red grapes
1/4 cup diced red onion

In a small cup, mix the chutney, orange juice, curry powder, ginger, and cumin. Place chops in a large plastic zip top bag and coat with chutney mixture. Marinate overnight in the refrigerator, shaking bag occasionally.

Preheat oven to 450∞. Brush a broiler pan with olive oil and place pork chops on it. Bake for 15 minutes or more until chops are done.

To make Tropical Fruit Salsa, in a cup stir together the lemon juice, zest, honey, cilantro, pepper sauce and cumin. Set aside.

In a medium bowl, gently toss the fruit and onion, pouring the lemon honey mixture over this and coating thoroughly.

Chill several hours and serve with Curried Pork Chops.

Yield: 4 servings, plus 2 cups salsa

Spicy Coconut Pork Chops

Guadeloupe

These are a big hit with the kids.

1/4 cup sweetened coconut flakes
1 small Serrano chili pepper, seeded and finely chopped (for children substitute a milder chili such as Poblano)
1 garlic clove, crushed
1/4 teaspoon cumin
1/2 teaspoon dried oregano
1/2 teaspoon dried rosemary
1/2 teaspoon dried thyme
1/2 teaspoon salt
freshly ground black pepper
4 (6-ounce) center-cut loin pork chops
1 tablespoon olive oil

Preheat oven to 450∞.

Combine all ingredients except ground pepper, oil, and pork in a large zip top plastic bag. Seal bag and shake vigorously.

Coat the chops lightly with the olive oil and brush remainder of oil on broiler pan. Place chops in bag with coconut mixture and shake until meat is completed covered.

Bake for 15 minutes, turning once until done. Season with black pepper to taste.

Yield: 4 servings

Ribs 101

Not all ribs are alike. There are several different types of ribs. Each serving is approximately 1 pound.

*Move ribs around on the grill to avoid hot spots and cook evenly.

*Cook ribs slowly over 325°to 350°heat for crunchy ribs with tender meat.

*To check for doneness, try moving the ribs back and forth after 1 1/2 hours of cooking.

*For extra flavor use different hardwoods on the fire.

*Brush marinades on during the last 15 minutes of grilling to avoid a scorched flavor, unless of course you like that.

*Use fresh citrus zest, lemon, lime, orange and even grapefruit to add high flavor without masking the taste of the pork or adding unnecessary calories.

*Fresh spices, rubs, and jerk seasoning add a new dimension to pork.

baby back ribs: This is a very meaty and tender center section of loin chops near to the spine. Cooking time is approximately 1 hour per pound for each rack.
spare ribs: Located from the belly of the pig, the meat is quite spare, however flavorful. Cooking time about 1/2 hour per pound.
country- style ribs: Located near the shoulder, these ribs are quite meaty and therefore a good idea to cook them first in water and then put on the fire. These are so full of meat that 1 pound will serve 2 to 3 people, instead of just 1.

Sizzling Ginger Lime Ribs with Mango-Guava Barbeque Sauce

St. Thomas

There are many roadside rib stands on this island, which produce excellent fare. This 3 step recipe will yield crunchy, yet tender ribs bursting with flavor. Plan to make extra for seconds.

1 pound baby back or spare ribs per serving/person, cut in 8-inch slabs

Ginger-Lime Rub
1 tablespoon freshly grated ginger root
1/2 teaspoon ground cumin
1/4 teaspoon cinnamon
2 tablespoons brown sugar
2 teaspoons salt
1 teaspoon lime zest

Preheat barbeque grill to approximately 350∞.

In a small bowl, combine all the ingredients for the Ginger-Lime Rub and place into a large zip top plastic bag.

Place the ribs cut in 8 inch slabs in the plastic bag, shaking and coating evenly with the rub. Press any remaining rub into the meat. Put on a large tray and refrigerate.

Habanero Rum Baste

As mentioned previously, sugary barbeque, sauces need to be applied towards the end of grilling to avoid scorched ribs with an unpleasant flavor.

1/2 small Serrano or Habanero pepper, seeded and minced.
1/4 cup dark rum
juice of 1 lime
1 cup vegetable broth
1 teaspoon olive oil

Combine all Habanero Rum Baste ingredients in a small bowl.

Have a large basting brush handy and baste consistently to retain moisture in ribs while they grill, every 10 or 15 minutes.

Mango Guava Barbeque Sauce:

2 tablespoons extra-virgin olive oil
1 small yellow onion, minced
1 cup fresh diced mango
3 tablespoons guava paste
juice of 2 limes
1 teaspoon fresh lime zest
2 tablespoons honey
1/2 teaspoon ground cumin
2 cloves garlic crushed
1/2 cup brown sugar
1 tablespoon tomato paste

Directions for Mango Guava Barbeque Sauce: heat the oil in a small saucepan, add the onion cooking until clear.

Whirl the mango, guava paste, lime juice, zest, honey, cumin, garlic, sugar, tomato paste, and the onions in a food processor until smooth.

Add the mango mixture to the onion and bring to a simmer. Cook until slightly thickened about 25 minutes.

To cook ribs:

Brush the preheated grill with olive oil.

Place the ribs on the grill, baste, and turn over with Habanero Rum Baste every 15 to 20 minutes. Be sure that the grill does not get too hot, as this is a slow-cooking process.

Approximately 15 minutes before grilling is done, baste the ribs with Mango Guava Barbeque Sauce, turning a couple of times. Serve with remaining sauce.

Caribbean Lamb
Trinidad

Lamb also makes a wonderful substitute for red meat.

4 (8-ounce) lean French-cut lamb chops
1/4 cup Jerk rub
1 tablespoon olive oil

Rub jerk mixture into the lamb and refrigerate for 1 hour.

Preheat oven to 425∞.

Coat a broiler pan with the olive oil and bake lamb for 25 minutes or preference.

Serve with rice.

Yield: 4 servings

Curried Lamb and Sweet Potato Stew

St. Croix

Very nice on chilly winter days.

3/4 pound lean boned leg of lamb, cut into 1-inch cubes
2 tablespoons olive oil, divided
1 tablespoon curry powder
1 teaspoon garam masala
1/2 cup minced yellow onion
1 clove garlic, minced
1/2 cup coconut milk (unsweetened)
1 cup chicken broth
1/2 cup vegetable broth
1/2 small Serrano pepper, seeded and minced
1 bay leaf
1/2 cup golden raisins
1 cup cauliflower florets
1/2 cup sliced carrot
3 cups cubed sweet potato
1 cup cubed white potato
3 cups hot cooked basmati rice
salt and pepper to taste

In a large deep skillet or soup pot, brown the lamb in 1 tablespoon of the olive oil. Remove from skillet and set aside.

In a small dry skillet gently heat the curry powder and garam masala until slightly browned and an aroma is released. Remove from heat.

In the same skillet used for the lamb, heat the remaining oil and add the onion and garlic, cooking until clear. Add the coconut milk, broths, spices, lamb, onion, garlic, peppers, raisins, and bay leaf. Bring to a boil, reducing to a simmer. After 40 minutes add remaining vegetables and cook until tender, about another 15 or 20 minutes. Remove from heat and allow to sit for 20 minutes, covered.

Spoon hot rice into bowls and top with Curried Lamb and Sweet Potato Stew.

Yield: 6 servings

Island Speak: *Yo check?*
Translation: You understand?

Keshi Yena

Curacao

Baked Gouda or Edam cheese is hollowed out and stuffed with a variety of fillings ranging from shrimp, chicken, or beef. Thrift and ingenuity was the name of the game in plantation days when supplies had to last from the visit of one ship to another. Hence, everything was put to clever use.

A bit of advice—never use a young soft cheese!

1 small yellow onion, minced
1 small garlic clove, minced
1/4 cup butter
1 1/2 pounds lean ground beef
1 green bell pepper, seeded and chopped
1/2 small Habanero or other fiery pepper, carefully
    seeded and minced
1 small stalk celery, finely chopped
2 medium firm tomatoes, peeled and chopped
1 small stalk celery, finely chopped
2 tablespoons fresh parsley, chopped
1 tablespoon capers
1/4 cup pimento olives, chopped
1/4 cup raisins
2 tablespoons ketchup
2 tablespoons relish or chopped gherkins
salt and pepper to taste
1 beaten egg
2 hard-boiled eggs, chopped
4-pound Edam or Gouda cheese

In a large deep frying pan, sauté the onions and garlic in the butter until clear. Crumble in ground beef, cooking for 1 minute, adding bell pepper, habanero pepper, and celery. Sauté for 5 additional minutes. Gently fold in remaining ingredients, except cheese and eggs; cook over low heat for 5 minutes. Remove from heat, pour into a colander, and run hot water over the mixture until most of the fat has been washed away.

Peel off the red wax covering from the cheese and carefully cut off the top, putting the "lid" aside for now. With a large spoon scoop out the cheese, leaving about a 1/2" shell. Submerge the shell and lid in cold water for one hour. Drain and pat dry. Grate approximately one cup of the cheese coarsely and fold into the beef. Spoon the beaten egg into the bottom of the cheese. Fill the cheese with the meat mixture halfway. Spoon the chopped egg over the meat and fill with remainder of the meat.

Preheat oven to 350∞. Generously grease a casserole with butter and place the cheese into it. Bake for 30 minutes, uncovered. Do not cook too long, as this will break down the protein in the cheese making it stringy. Five minutes before removing cheese, put lid on the top and return to oven.

Remove from casserole and cut into thick slices.

Yield: 8 servings

West Indian Meat Pie

St. Thomas, U.S. Virgin Islands

This recipe had its beginnings with my ex-husband's grandmother, who lived nearly her entire life on St. Thomas. Over the years, I modified it and it changed once more. A slightly different version can be found in "A Taste of the Virgin Islands."

One single deep dish pie shell, slightly under-baked and cooled
1 pound extra-lean ground beef
1 small green bell pepper
1 small red bell pepper
1 habanero or other equally fiery pepper, carefully seeded and minced
1/4 cup pimento stuffed olives
1/2 teaspoon coriander
1/4 teaspoon nutmeg
1/2 teaspoon thyme
1/2 teaspoon cumin
4 tablespoons cider vinegar
1/2 small can tomato paste
1/2 cup water
1 cup sharp cheddar cheese, grated
salt and pepper to taste

In a large skillet, brown meat, adding all ingredients except water, vinegar, tomato paste, cheese and pie shell. Drain and rinse meat mixture in a colander, using hot water. This will wash away most of the fat, leaving the flavor. Return meat to skillet adding remaining ingredients except cheese. Simmer for about 15 minutes, until thickened.

Preheat oven to 350∞. Fill piecrust with mixture, sprinkling cheddar evenly across the top.
Protect edges of pie from burning by covering edges only with aluminum foil. Bake until slightly bubbly and light golden brown on top.

Yield: 4 to 6 servings

Jamaican Blackened Beef

Ocho Rios

Mix a tablespoon of Cointreau Mango Chutney along with 1/2 of a small seeded habanero pepper, minced into half a cup of mayonnaise for a delicious dip for this savory beef.

1 small Habanero pepper seeded and minced
2 tablespoons dark rum
4 tablespoons olive oil
1 2 pound beef filet or tenderloin
1 tablespoon salt
1 teaspoon allspice
1/4 teaspoon nutmeg
1/4 teaspoon cinnamon
1 tablespoon onion powder
1/4 teaspoon ground mustard
1 teaspoon ground black pepper
1 teaspoon thyme
1 tablespoon brown sugar

Preheat oven to 325∞.

In a small mortar and pestle, combine the habanero pepper with the dark rum and 2 tablespoons of the olive oil. Baste the filet generously with this.

In a large zip type plastic bag, toss all the dry ingredients. Place the beef inside the bag, seal, and shake until well coated.

Pour a couple of tablespoons of the olive oil into a heavy skillet and turn the heat up high. Sear and seal the meat on both sides for 1 1/2 to 2 minutes. Remove from heat and bake in oven for 12 minutes.

Slice thinly and serve at once with rice and fried plantains.

Yield: 6 servings

Pork Chops with Fire-Roasted Pepper Sauce
Anguilla

The island's main attractions are it's glittering, endless beaches set into a translucent aquamarine sea. Each beach is completely different from the other. Some are romantically deserted, others lined with restaurants, bars, calm waves and frantically wild surf, long beaches for walking and even dunes.

4 boneless pork chops about 6 ounces, one-inch thick
2 tablespoon sea salt
1 teaspoon cayenne pepper
1 teaspoon cumin
1/2 teaspoon thyme
1/2 teaspoon allspice
cold water

sauce:
2 medium sweet red bell peppers, sliced in quarters and seeded
1 medium Habanero pepper, sliced in half and seeded
1 medium yellow onion, peeled and quartered
4 garlic cloves, peeled
1/2 cup fresh cilantro, stems removed and coarsely chopped
1/2 teaspoon sea salt
1/2 teaspoon freshly ground pepper
1/4 cup dark rum
2 tablespoons olive oil

olive oil for brushing chops and vegetables

Fill a large glass bowl 1/2 full with cold water and stir in 2 tablespoons sea salt, cayenne pepper, cumin, thyme, and allspice. Submerge the chops, adding more water if necessary. Refrigerate for one hour.

In a large roasting pan, place the sweet and hot peppers, onion and garlic, brushing generously with olive oil. Place under the broiler and lightly brown. Remove from pan and place on a ceramic plate, allowing cooling. Place vegetables, onion garlic mixture along with remaining ingredients into a food processor and puree. Transfer to a small saucepan and gently heat through, keeping warm.

Remove chops from salt water and dry with white paper towels. Brush lightly with olive oil and grill over medium heat for about 11 minutes until just a tiny bit of pink remains in the middle.

Serve at once with Fire-Roasted Pepper Sauce and garlic mashed potatoes.

Yield: 4 servings

Aromatic Coffee and Pepper Filet
St. Barths

The first time I flew into St. Barth's, the airport seemed to be located in a cow pasture. This tiny 10-mile square island boasts some of the finest cuisine in the Caribbean, both traditional and innovative. Serve the following with a crisp Sauvignon Blanc.

4 six to eight once filet of tenderloin
2 tablespoons olive oil
1 garlic clove crushed
3 tablespoons unflavored freshly ground coffee beans
3 tablespoons coarsely ground black pepper
1/2 teaspoon ground cumin

Preheat a barbeque grill to high heat.

Mix the olive oil with the garlic clove and generously brush the meat. Place the coffee, pepper, and ground cumin in a large plastic bag. Add the filets one at time, hold tightly closed and shake until the meat is well coated. Press any extra seasoning into the meat.

Grill over high heat, turning once for about 4 to 5 minutes per side or until desired. Remove from heat and serve with a fresh green salad and baked potato.

Yield: 4 servings

Virgin Island Daube Meat

St. Thomas

This pot roast got its name Daube from the way that West Indians cooked their meats. For lack of an oven, food was cooked over a fire in an iron pot and daubed with plenty of sauce.

1 three to five pound pot roast
2 tablespoons olive oil
1 tablespoon sea salt
1 tablespoon coarsely ground black pepper
1/4 teaspoon nutmeg
1/4 teaspoon mace
1/2 teaspoon thyme
1 large onion, chopped
1/2 stalk celery, minced
1 tablespoon freshly chopped parsley
1 large ripe tomato, chopped
1 tablespoon vinegar
water

In a large deep, stew pot, brown the meat on all sides with the olive oil. Add remaining ingredients and cover meat with the water. Simmer until meat is tender, but not coarse and dried out.

Serve with baked sweet potatoes and fried plantains.

Yield: 6 to 8 servings

Island Speak: Yeah, mon.
Translation: Yes, I agree.

Luquillo Roast Pork
Puerto Rico

La isla bonita, the beautiful island of Puerto Rico. Roast pork is as indigenous to Puerto Ricans as Jerk is to Jamaicans. The secret to tender Puerto Rican pork is in the liberal use of the adobo or marinade. Utilizing a mortar and pestle contributes to the authenticity of this recipe.

1/2 cup olive oil
15 garlic cloves, peeled, and crushed
2 tablespoons oregano
3 tablespoons coarse salt
1/4 cup coarsely ground black pepper
1 tablespoon coriander
1 teaspoon cumin
1/4 cup Seville (bitter) orange juice—found in Hispanic groceries
1 tablespoon annatto seed
1 leg of pork, approximately 10 pounds

In the large mortar and pestle, combine 1 tablespoon of the olive oil along with the garlic, oregano, salt, pepper, coriander and cumin—pounding in an up and down motion until a smooth paste is formed. Stir in the bitter orange juice. Refrigerate.

Heat the remaining olive oil in a small sauce pan and add the annatto seeds. Keep over low heat until the oil is turns orange. Remove from heat. Strain and discard the seeds.

Place the pork leg in a deep roasting pan with the skin up. Remove any excess fat. Use a sharp knife and make long diagonal incisions through the skin about 1 1/2 inches deep to keep it from blowing up during roasting. Take small amounts of the adobo paste and fill the incisions.

Baste the leg generously with the olive oil and refrigerate overnight.

Preheat oven to 350∞. Roast the meat until a meat thermometer reads 185°upon insertion. Baste the meat continuously with the seasoned drippings.

Serve with roast yams, sweet potatoes, garlic potatoes, and rice.

Yield: 8 servings

Did you know?: Pork is higher in B-complex vitamins that red meat or chicken. Contains a good source of phosphorus, zinc, and potassium. Always thoroughly, cook pork to kill trichinae. Of note, the ancient Jews avoided pork, which inevitably became a protection against parasites. Over the years, pork has been specially bred to reduce its fat content.

Purchasing: Choose the tenderest cuts which come from the back (loin), i.e. fillets, roasts, and chops.

Storing: All meats of course should be refrigerated. Ground pork keeps for a couple of days, chops for 2 to 3 days, roasts for about 3 days. Unprepared meat may be frozen for up to 6 months.

Batabano (ground turtle)
Grand Cayman

About 5 years ago, while on a photo shoot on Grand Cayman, we visited the local turtle farm, quite a venerable enterprise. Turtles are farmed here and sold for their meat. The hatchlings are tiny and will fit in the palm of a child's hand. A full grown turtle has a giant head the size of an adult human being.

Ground hamburger or pork may be guiltlessly substituted with good results.

1 medium yellow onion, minced
1 clove garlic, peeled and minced
1/2 small habanero pepper, seeded and minced
2 large red sweet bell peppers, seeded and chopped
2 pounds ground beef or turtle
1 cup water
1 small ripe tomato, diced
1/2 cup pimento stuffed olives
1/2 cup capers
1/2 cup dark raisins
4 tablespoons tomato paste
1 tablespoon freshly ground pepper
1/2 teaspoon celery salt
1/4 teaspoon cumin
1/4 teaspoon oregano
2 tablespoons Worcestershire sauce
2 tablespoons light or dark rum
1 tablespoon vinegar
1 tablespoon olive oil
salt to taste

Sauté the onion, garlic, and peppers in the olive oil until the onion is just clear. Set aside

Brown the ground meat and drain. Place the meat in a colander and rinse with hot water to rinse any excess fat. Add all remaining ingredients including the onion mixture to pan along with 1 cup of water. Stir well and simmer for about 35 minutes over low heat.

Serve at once with rice and salad.

Yield: 4 servings

Citrus-Glazed Pork Tenderloin

Barbados

Many of the upscale hotels in Barbados have imported chefs from the United States and Europe to tempt and maintain their clientele. Gourmet dining is represented by beef, veal, or seafood with finely diversified sauces.

2 pork tenderloins approximately one pound each
olive oil

sauce:
1 tablespoon frozen orange juice concentrate
2 tablespoons ketchup
1 teaspoon freshly grated orange zest
1 tablespoon apple cider vinegar
1 teaspoon habanero hot sauce or any other good and fiery sauce
1 teaspoon sesame oil
2 teaspoons soy sauce
1 teaspoon cumin

In a large glass bowl, combine all ingredients for the sauce and blend well. Add pork, cover, and refrigerate overnight.

Remove pork from marinade and grill over low to medium heat until the tenderloins reach an internal temperature of approximately 155∞, about 25 minutes.

Remove from grill and slice. Goes nicely with garlicky mashed potatoes and string beans.

Yield: 4 servings

Baked Stuffed Papaya

Jamaica

Not all food from Jamaica is jerked. Serve this delicious fruit and meat dish on a blustery winter day to evoke Caribbean memories. Green papaya is quite starchy and similar to other root tubers.

2 tablespoons olive oil
1 small yellow onion, minced
1 garlic clove, minced
1 small green bell pepper, seeded and minced
1/2 small Habanero pepper, seeded and minced
1/2 pound lean ground beef
1/2 pound ground lamb
2 tablespoons tomato paste
1 tablespoon Tabasco sauce
1 tablespoon cider vinegar
2 tablespoons capers
1 5 lb. green papaya or several small ones if not available, halved and seeded
4 ounces extra-sharp aged cheddar cheese
salt and pepper to taste

Preheat oven to 350∞.

In a large skillet, heat the oil and sauté the onion, garlic, and peppers for 3 to 4 minutes. Add in the ground meats until cooked. Drain any excess fat.

Stir in the tomato paste, Tabasco, vinegar, and capers. Carefully ladle in the meat mixture into the hollowed out papayas and place in a shallow baking dish. Pour in about 1 inch of water, baking for an hour. Watch carefully so the tops do not blacken. May be covered intermittently with foil.

Grate the cheddar and sprinkle liberally over the top of the meat shells. Serve at once.

Yield: approximately 6 servings

Pepperpot

St. Kitts

Originally, from Guyana, this stew has spread to the Caribbean islands. Cassareep gives it a well-known unique flavor. Cassareep comes from grated raw cassava, which is pressed for juice and then reduced by boiling. This may be purchased in West Indian markets.

2 pounds lean pork, cubed
2 pounds lean beef, cubed
1 pound salt pork, chopped
2 tablespoon olive oil
1 large onion, chopped
2 garlic cloves, crushed
1 tablespoon fresh thyme, coarsely chopped
3 habanero or other hot chili peppers, tied in cheese cloth
1/2 cup Cassareep
salt and pepper to taste

Brown the meat in 2 tablespoons of olive oil on all sides in a large stock or soup pot. Cover meat with cold water and add all other ingredients except hot chilies. Simmer for 2 hours until meat is cooked. Add the hot peppers and cook for another 30 minutes.

Serve with Johnny Cakes or pita bread.

Yield: 4 to 6 servings

Cha, Cha, Cha Chickens

Poultry is simple to prepare, versatile and low in calories. The variety of taste sensations is endless.

Chicken has always been a part of Caribbean cooking. Join our culinary tour with Virgin Islands Pirate Stew, Montego Bay Jerked Chicken, Crisp Honey Cinnamon Chicken and others.

Nothing seems to taste better than chicken cooked in coconut milk and if it is cooked in curry so much the better. Of course, nothing beats a trip to the islands to sample first hand all the delicious chicken dishes!

Virgin Islands Pirate Stew

St. Croix

Legends abound in the Caribbean about pirates, their buried treasure and shipwrecks. 'Three dead men and a bottle of rum . . .'

1 pound boneless chicken thighs
1 pound boneless chicken breast
2 bacon strips, cooked and crumbled
1 small yellow onion, minced
1 stalk celery, minced
1 tablespoon fresh grated ginger
1 large carrot, thinly sliced
1 cup frozen peas, cooked
1/2 habanero or other fiery pepper, seeded and minced
1/4 cup frozen pineapple juice concentrate
1/4 cup tamari or soy sauce
2 garlic cloves crushed
1/4 cup dark rum
1 cup water
1 cup basmati rice, brown or white
water

Put all ingredients except rice in a large soup pot. Bring to boil, cover and lower to a simmer.

Cook for 25 minutes. Add the rice and 2 cups additional water. Cook another 20 minutes.

YIELD: 4 SERVINGS

Antiguan Chicken and Potato Croquettes
Antigua

This dish is also a nice appetizer. Make the croquettes just a little smaller ad skewer with toothpicks.

1 pound cooked chopped chicken
1 cup mashed potatoes
1/3 cup fresh chopped parsley
1 clove garlic, minced
1 small onion, minced
1 celery stalk, minced
1/2 cup seasoned breadcrumbs
3 eggs, beaten
1 teaspoon habanero pepper sauce
oil for frying
salt and pepper to taste

Combine all ingredients except for the oil and form into balls the size of ping pongs—flatten slightly.

In a heavy skillet, heat the oil to 350 degrees, drop in the balls and fry until golden brown.

Drain on paper towels and serve with Hot Banana Chutney. Season with salt and pepper.

YIELD: Enough for 4 to 6

Montego Bay Jerked Chicken

Jamaica

Chicken wings may be substituted for the chicken drumsticks. Allow at least an hour for the chicken to marinate and absorb the spices.

12 chicken drumsticks or 36 chicken wings
1/2 medium onion, minced
1/2 cup scallions, finely chopped
1 habanero pepper, seeded and finely chopped
1 tablespoon orange zest
2 garlic cloves, crushed
1 tablespoon fresh, grated ginger
1/4 cup fresh lime juice
1 tablespoon apple cider vinegar
1/4 cup honey
1/4 cup brown sugar
1 tablespoon fresh chopped thyme
2 teaspoons Worcestershire
2 tablespoons olive oil
2 teaspoons ground cinnamon
2 teaspoons ground nutmeg
1 1/2 tablespoons ground allspice
2 teaspoons fresh ground pepper

Put all ingredients in a food processor except the chicken, until paste forms.

Rub mixture onto the chicken and marinate 1 to 3 hours.

Barbecue chicken on a hot grill until tender. For variation, soak mesquite or other hardwood chips in cold water for a half hour and scatter over barbecue coals.

YIELD: SERVES 4

Did you know? The first chicken was domesticated in southern Asia over 4000 years ago? Chickens are eaten after they are six weeks old. Broilers are seven weeks and weigh between 2 1/2 and 4 pounds. Roasting chickens are 10 weeks and weigh over 4 pounds. Choose air-chilled chicken because water-chilled chicken contains between 3% and 5% water, not such a good buy. Chicken is high in protein, B6 and niacin.

Purchasing: Larger chickens are a better buy as there is more meat in proportion to bones. Whole chicken costs less than cut up chicken.

Plantain-Stuffed Chicken in Peanut Crust

St. Martin, French West Indies

Plantains are in the banana family and are delicious when cooked. I find them a little firmer than bananas and therefore easier to work with.

4 pounds boneless, skinless chicken breasts
1 1/2 cups shelled, roasted peanuts
1/2 cup firmly packed brown sugar
1/4 cup seasoned breadcrumbs
oil for frying
1 1/2 large ripe plantains, peeled and sliced like a banana
1/2 teaspoon vanilla
1/4 cup Cointreau Mango Chutney
3 eggs beaten
salt and pepper to taste
light oil for frying

Lay each chicken breast flat after washing and drying. With a sharp knife, slice down the side to make a pocket for plantain stuffing.

In a food processor, grind the peanuts to powder. Mix with the brown sugar and breadcrumbs.

In a deep frying pan, heat the oil over medium heat. Fry plantain slices on each side, until barely golden. They will continue to cook later with the chicken. Drain on paper towels.

Mix the vanilla with the chutney and place 2 tablespoons in the center of each chicken pocket. Divide the plantain equally and stuff the chicken.

Dip the chicken in the egg mixture, then dredge in the peanut crust. For the calorie conscious, you may bake the breasts for 35 to 40 minutes. Breasts may also be fried in vegetable oil until golden. Drain on paper towels.

YIELD: 4 SERVINGS

Guadeloupe Chicken
Guadeloupe

This delightful light and fruity recipe bursts with tropical flavors such as kiwi, coconut, mango, pineapple and almonds.

1 pound boneless, skinless chicken breasts
1 pound boneless skinless chicken thighs
1 tablespoon olive oil
1 small onion, minced
1 stalk celery, minced
2 cloves garlic, minced
1 tablespoon fresh ginger
1 16 ounce can coconut milk, the reduced fat version may be used
1/2 teaspoon cinnamon
1 tablespoon soy sauce
1/2 teaspoon almond extract
1 cup fresh pineapple, chopped
1 cup fresh, slightly unripe kiwi, peeled and diced
1 cup fresh, slightly unripe mango, chopped
1 large ripe plantain, peeled, sliced and fried until golden
1/2 cup unsweetened fresh or packaged coconut
2/3 cup crushed almonds
salt and pepper to taste

In deep skillet, brown the chicken on all sides in the olive oil until golden. Remove chicken and cube.

Add the onion, garlic, celery, ginger and sauté until the onions are clear.

Return chicken to skillet, add the coconut milk, cinnamon, soy sauce and almond extract. Simmer covered for 25 minutes. Add pineapple and cook for another 5 or 6 minutes. Fold in mango, cook for one minute. Cook kiwi for one additional minute.

Arrange in deep serving platter, with plantains used as a garnish. Sprinkle with nuts and coconut.

Serve over rice. Season with salt and pepper.

YIELD: 4 SERVINGS

Thairibbean Spicy Chicken

St. Marteen, Netherlands Antilles

A number of Thai/Caribbean restaurants have popped up suddenly in the Caribbean with much success. I particularly like the spiciness of this recipe served with fresh pineapple.

1 3 to 4 pound roasting chicken, cut into pieces
2 tablespoons peanut butter
3 tablespoons soy sauce
2 tablespoons dark brown sugar
juice of 2 limes
1 small onion, minced
3 cloves garlic, minced
1 Thai pepper, seeded and minced
1 tablespoon fresh grated ginger
1 teaspoon fresh lemon zest
3 tablespoons fresh vegetable oil
2 tablespoons fresh cracked pepper

Make a marinade of the above except chicken by placing in a food processor. Rub well into the chicken and refrigerate for 3 hours.

Fire up the barbecue grill, and roast slowly over low heat. Baste chicken with marinade to keep from drying out.

YIELD: 4 SERVINGS

Puerto Rican Stew Chicken with Saffron and Cinnamon

Puerto Rico

This dish can easily be made ahead of time. Serve with white rice and plantains.

3 tablespoons vegetable oil
6 saffron threads
2 tablespoons fresh cilantro, chopped finely
2 teaspoons cinnamon
1 small onion, chopped
2 cloves garlic, crushed
3 sweet red bell peppers, finely chopped
1 Serrano pepper, seeded and minced
4 pounds of cut up roasting chicken
1 cup chicken stock
1/2 cup vegetable stock
1/2 small can tomato paste
1 pound fresh chopped tomatoes
1/2 cup black olives, pitted and chopped
salt and pepper to taste

Heat oil in small frying pan. Add saffron, cilantro, cinnamon, onion, garlic and all the peppers, mild and hot. Sauté until the onions are clear. Allow cooling and then rub this mixture onto the chicken. Refrigerate for 2 hours.

In deep skillet, combine the stocks with the tomato paste and bring to a low simmer. Add the chicken and cook for 30 minutes until chicken is tender.

Add the tomatoes and olives for the last 15 minutes. Season with salt and pepper.

YIELD: 4 TO 6 SERVINGS

Barbados Chicken with Breadfruit and Pear

Barbados

Potatoes may be substituted for the breadfruit. Serve with an ice-cold sparkling wine.

1 tablespoon vegetable oil
1 large white onion, minced
1 large sweet red pepper, cut in slivers
2 jalapeno peppers, chopped
3 cloves garlic, minced
1 teaspoon fresh lime zest
juice of one lemon and one lime
1 teaspoon paprika
1 teaspoon fresh chopped thyme
1/2 teaspoon allspice
1/2 teaspoon nutmeg
2 tablespoons fresh cilantro, finely chopped
2 pounds chicken drumsticks
1 pound peeled and cubed breadfruit
2 pears, peeled, cored and diced
1 teaspoon fresh lime zest

Heat vegetable oil in small frying pan. Sauté onion, peppers, and garlic. In blender, combine citrus juice and zest, onion mixture, paprika, thyme, allspice, nutmeg and cilantro.

In glass baking dish, arrange chicken, breadfruit and pear. Pour blender mixture over the top. Refrigerate 3 hours the bake at 375 degrees for 45 minutes until chicken is tender.

YIELD: 4 SERVINGS

Shipwreck Chicken Stew

Virgin Gorda, British Virgin Islands

The treasure in this chicken lies in its delightful coconut curry base.

1/2 teaspoon turmeric
1 teaspoon cumin
1/4 teaspoon coriander
1/2 teaspoon nutmeg
2 tablespoons oil
1 medium onion, minced
2 cloves garlic, minced
1 teaspoon fresh grated ginger
1 small red bell pepper, thinly sliced
4 tablespoons sugar
1/2 cup chicken stock
1 cup coconut milk
6 boneless chicken breasts
1 large carrot, thinly sliced
1 package frozen peas
1 teaspoon chili powder
1/4 cup fresh parsley, finely chopped
1/2 teaspoon thyme

In a small frying pan, heat the spices until they give off a delightful aroma. Do not burn them. Add the oil and sauté the onion, garlic, ginger and the peppers.

In large deep skillet, place the sugar and heat until the sugar browns and melts.

Add chicken stock and coconut milk along with the chicken and the onion pepper mixture. Simmer for 20 minutes. Add all remaining ingredients and continue to cook until vegetables and chicken are tender.

Serve with Orange Coconut Rice.

YIELD: 4 TO 6 SERVINGS

Paradise Fowl

St. Thomas

Our longtime housekeeper, a true St. Thomian often used leftover chicken or turkey to make this tasty dish.

2 tablespoons oil
3 cloves garlic, crushed
1 medium onion, minced
1 sweet red pepper, diced
1/2 teaspoon nutmeg
1/2 teaspoon cardamom
1 tablespoon paprika
2 pounds cooked chicken or other fowl removed from the bone
1/2 habanero pepper, seeded and minced
1 1/2 cups vegetable stock
1/2 cup green pimento-stuffed olives cut in half
2 tablespoons brown sugar
2 tablespoons fresh lemon juice
1/2 cup heavy cream
2 cups cooked white or brown rice

In a large, deep skillet heat the oil and sauté the garlic, onion, sweet pepper and spices until the onion is clear.

Add all other ingredients except the cream and rice. Bring to a simmer for 20 minutes. Stir in rice and cream; serve at once.

YIELD: 4 TO 6 SERVINGS

Cuban Papaya Chicken and Rice
Cuba

Cuban food is enjoying an ever-increasing popularity as is evidenced by the great number of Cuban restaurants in Miami and Puerto Rico. Try this one at your next dinner party.

3 tablespoons olive oil
1/2 teaspoon coriander
1 teaspoon chili powder
1/4 teaspoon nutmeg
1/4 teaspoon mace
1 teaspoon cayenne pepper
1 teaspoon grated ginger
2 garlic cloves, crushed
1 small onion, minced
1 cup fresh papaya, peeled, seeded and diced
1 cup fresh pineapple, cored and diced
1 small green apple, cored and diced
2 pounds boneless, skinless chicken thighs
1/4 cup fresh lime juice
1 tablespoon fresh cilantro, chopped
1 tablespoon fresh thyme, chopped
1/2 cup raisins
1/2 cup sweetened condensed milk
1 cup sour cream
cooked white rice

Heat oil over low heat, add spices and heat until an aroma is emitted from the spices. Add the ginger, garlic and onion; sauté until onions are clear.

In a blender, process the papaya, pineapple, and the apple until smooth. Pour mixture into the skillet with the onion and spices.

Add chicken, lime juice, cilantro and thyme simmering for 20 minutes.

Add raisins, cooking an additional 10 to 12 minutes over low heat.

Stir in milk and sour cream and remove from heat.

Serve over cooked white rice.

YIELD: 4 TO 6 SERVINGS

Did you know? Papaya trees bear fruit all year round? Papain, an enzyme that tenderizes meat is made from unripe papaya. It is also used for medicinal purposes and in chewing gum. There are about 50 types of papayas. The fruit can weigh anywhere from a few ounces to several pounds. The skin is inedible, the fruit a rich orange color with a musky melon-like flavor, and the center contains edible black peppery seeds. Papaya is an excellent source of vitamin C, supplying potassium and vitamin in substantial amounts a well.

Purchasing: Choose fruits that are not green and have either a yellow or orange skin. Some black spots are fine. Fruits will yield slightly to touch, but should not be mushy.

Storing: Ripe papaya may be refrigerated for several days, but should be eaten quickly. Do not freeze. Unripe fruit may be put in a brown paper bag to hasten ripening.

Crisp Honey Cinnamon Chicken
Cozumel

Serve with Grilled Pineapple, Avocado, and Onion Salad at your next summer barbecue or picnic.

4 pounds chicken drumsticks
five spice powder:
1 tablespoon cinnamon
1/2 teaspoon allspice
1/2 teaspoon nutmeg
1 teaspoon chili powder
1 teaspoon cayenne pepper
salt and pepper to taste
1 cup honey
3 tablespoons sesame oil
juice and zest of one lemon
1 lemon, quartered
peanut oil for frying

Wash and rinse chicken under cold running water. Rub chicken with spices salt and pepper.

In a small bowl, combine honey, sesame oil, lemon juice and zest. Place chicken in a glass baking dish and pour honey mixture over the top. Refrigerate for 3 hours.

Heat oil in deep skillet and fry chicken until golden brown. Drain on paper towels and season with additional salt and pepper if necessary.

Squeeze lemon over the chicken. In addition, nice served with Pigeon Peas and Rice.

YIELD: 4 TO 6 SERVINGS

Island Speak: *When fowl gib party him no ax mongoose. When cockroachy gib dance him no ax fowl.*
Translation: Steer clear of your enemies; pick your friends very carefully.

Arroz Con Pollo

Puerto Rico

Chicken and Rice is probably one of the most popular dishes in the Hispanic Caribbean repertoire.

1/4 cup olive oil
2 garlic cloves, minced
2 tablespoons chopped jalapeno peppers
1 large red bell pepper, minced
1 large green bell pepper, minced
1 medium onion, minced
4 saffron threads
1/2 teaspoon cumin
1/2 teaspoon oregano
2 pounds assorted boneless and skinless chicken breasts and thighs
1/2 cup dry sherry
1 cup vegetable broth
1/2 cup water
1 tablespoon Worcestershire sauce
3 tablespoons cider vinegar
1 cup pigeon peas or black-eyed peas, soaked and boiled
1 cup white rice

In a large skillet, heat oil, garlic, peppers, onion, herbs and spices.

Add chicken and brown on all sides. Pour into a glass casserole dish with a cover. Combine the sherry, broths, and any remaining ingredients and pour over the chicken. Mix the rice and peas together and sprinkle over chicken and vegetables.

Bake at 350 for 45 minutes until rice has absorbed the liquid.

YIELD: 4 SERVINGS

Aruba Chicken Mango Casserole

Aruba

Aruba is a truly lovely island with gorgeous beaches and pristine villages. The chef at one of the premier restaurants in town shared this with me. Here is my version.

1 cup peeled diced mango
1/2 cup white wine
1/4 cup brown sugar
1/2 cup chicken stock
1 large onion, minced
2 cloves garlic, minced
1 teaspoon allspice
juice and zest of one lime
2 cups cooked white rice
1 cup frozen peas, thawed
1 cup frozen corn kernels, thawed
2 large carrots, thinly sliced
2 pounds cooked chicken meat, de-boned, skinned and cubed
1 cup buttered toasted bread crumbs

In food processor blend mango, wine, sugar, chicken stock, onion, garlic, allspice and lime juice and zest until smooth.

In a buttered covered casserole dish, layer rice, then vegetables, and then chicken, pouring mango puree over the top. Spread breadcrumbs and bake at 350 degrees covered for 30 minutes. Take the cover off and bake until slightly browned.

YIELD: 4 TO 6 SERVINGS

Deserted Island Bird

St. Lucia

This recipe is perfect for those surprise visits from in laws! Simple, fast and extremely elegant!

6 boneless skinless chicken breasts
1/2 cup Dijon-style mustard
1 cup sour cream
1/4 cup white wine
fresh cracked pepper

In a large glass baking dish, spread out the chicken breasts.

In a small bowl, combine all other ingredients.

Spoon this mixture over the chicken and sprinkle with the cracked pepper.

Cover with foil and bake at 350 degrees for 35 to 40 minutes. Remove foil for the last 10 minutes.

YIELD: 6 SERVINGS

Havana Hen
Miami

1/4 cup annatto oil
1 small onion, minced
2 cloves garlic, crushed
1/2 cup dry sherry
3 tablespoons brown sugar
1/4 cup chopped pimentos
2 tablespoons chopped fresh cilantro
4 pounds mixed chicken parts, legs, breasts, etc.
2 large potatoes, peeled and cubed
3/4 cup frozen corn kernels

In large skillet heat the annatto oil and add the onion, garlic, sherry, brown sugar, pimento, and cilantro. Sauté until the onion is clear.

Place the chicken, potato, and corn in a glass casserole dish, pouring the annatto mixture evenly over the top.

Bake covered with foil at 325 degrees for 40 minutes until chicken and potatoes are tender.

YIELD: 4 TO 6 SERVINGS

Did you know? Tamarind trees are indigenous to India and attain heights of 80 feet. A relative of the Carob tree, it grows in sub-tropical and tropical climates. Widely used in Asian and Caribbean cooking, the fruit is very sour and bitter. Too much can stimulate a laxative effect. Good source of potassium, magnesium, thiamine and iron.

Purchasing: One can purchase the pods in ethnic groceries, peel and boil down the pulp. Much easier to purchase the paste in a jar or frozen.

Storing: Room temperature is fine, but I prefer to refrigerate or freeze.

Tamarind Ginger Chicken

Jamaica

This Jamaican inspired dish mingles the spiciness of jerk with the tartness of fruit and the sweetness of honey.

1 three to four pound roasting chicken
1 cup jerk marinade (see Monte go Bay Jerked Chicken)
2 tablespoons tamarind paste
1/2 cup Cointreau Mango Chutney
1 tablespoon tamarind paste
1 tablespoon freshly grated ginger
juice and zest of one lime
1/4 cup honey

Preparation: Split chicken down the middle and marinate with 1/2 cup of the jerk marinade for 3 hours in the refrigerator.

Pre-heat barbecue to low even temperature. Remove chicken from marinade and place on a plate. In a small bowl combine remaining marinade with chutney, tamarind, ginger lime and honey. Roast chicken slowly on grill, basting continuously. Serve with baked breadfruit, fried plantains, and rice.

YIELD: 4 SERVINGS

Chicken Roasting 101

*Many of these chicken recipes can have their calorie content reduced by roasting the chicken either on a barbeque or broiler pan. The fat can then drip off and be discarded. Use the sauces as a basting marinade or serve over accompanying rice.

*Buy a roasting chicken as opposed to a broiler or fryer. These chickens have more meat and will be moister.

*Roast first at a high temperature (450∞) then lower to 350∞. This will keep the chicken from being too dry.

Tropical Chicken
with Apricots and Kiwi
Cancun

This dish gets its flavor boost from Chunky Kiwi Tomato Relish and aromatic spices.

1/2 teaspoon cumin
1/2 teaspoon coriander
1/2 teaspoon turmeric
1/2 teaspoon cayenne pepper
1/2 teaspoon nutmeg
1/2 teaspoon cinnamon
1 teaspoon fresh cracked pepper
1 1/2 cups chicken broth
1 cup vegetable broth
1 cup Basmati rice
1 cup dried apricots, well-chopped
2 tablespoons olive oil
4 boneless, skinless chicken breasts
1 large red onion, coarsely chopped
2 cloves garlic, crushed
2/3 cup Chunky Kiwi Tomato Relish
2 tablespoons fresh cilantro, chopped

In a large skillet, combine all the spices and heat until slightly browned and their aroma released.

Pour in 1 cup vegetable broth and 1 cup chicken broth plus the rice and apricots. Cook until rice has absorbed all the liquid.

Sauté the chicken, onions, and garlic in the oil until the onions are clear. Add the chutney and leftover chicken broth and cook until chicken is tender.

Toss the cilantro into the rice and serve the chicken onto a bed of the rice.

YIELD: 4 SERVINGS

Spicy Curried Chicken with Chickpeas and Rice
Trinidad

This dish belies its East Indian overtones, probably having traveled up the chain of islands from Trinidad. I gave it somewhat more of a Virgin Island flavor by adding sweet potato and rum.

1/4 cup melted butter
2 pounds boneless, skinless breasts of chicken
2 tablespoons curry powder
2 cloves garlic, crushed
1/2 cup scallions, finely chopped
1 tablespoon fresh grated ginger
1 tablespoon Asian pickled ginger slices
1/2 cup sliced carrots
1 pound white potatoes, peeled and diced
1 pound sweet potatoes, peeled and diced
1/2 cup coconut milk
1/4 cup dark rum
1 tablespoon habanero hot sauce, to taste
1 1/2 cups cooked chickpeas
salt and fresh cracked pepper to taste

Sauté the chicken in half the butter slowly for 10 minutes. In another pan, using medium to high heat, dry roast the curry for 1 1/2 minutes. Add remaining butter, garlic, scallions, gingers, and carrots.

In a deep skillet, cover the potatoes with water and bring to a boil. Cook until just barely soft. Drain all the water and substitute the liquid with the coconut milk and rum. Add chicken mixture to this and simmer slowly for 20 minutes until chicken is tender. Stir in hot sauce and chickpeas

Serve with Down Island Chewy Cornbread. Season with salt and pepper.

YIELD: 4 SERVINGS

Island Speak: Any dirty water cool copper. Translation: A poor substitute is absolutely better than nothing. If it puts out the fire, who cares if it's dirty?

Virgin Islands Chicken in Rum Ginger Sauce

St. Croix

This unusual dish goes well over something neutral such as pasta or white rice.

3 pounds boneless, skinless chicken thighs (white meat may be substituted, but the dark has a richer flavor
1 cup golden rum
1/2 cup light soy sauce
1/4 cup melted butter
1 large white onion, finely chopped
3 cloves garlic, crushed
1 green bell pepper, slivered
1 fiery chili pepper such as a habanero, seeded and minced
1 large carrot, thinly sliced
1 1/2 tablespoons freshly grated ginger
2 teaspoons cornstarch
1/2 cup crushed pineapple, fresh or canned
1/2 cup currants

Soak chicken in the rum and soy sauce for 4 hours in refrigerator.

Remove chicken reserving rum mixture. Carefully brown the chicken in butter, adding the onion, garlic, peppers, and carrots. Finally, add the ginger cooking over low heat for one minute.

Preheat oven to 350 degrees. In a small glass bowl, stir the cornstarch into the soy and rum mixture. Place chicken and vegetables into a glass baking dish with pineapple and currants on the top. Pour the rum mixture over this.

Cover with foil and bake 35 minutes.

YIELD: 4 SERVINGS

Island Turkey Burgers with Blue Cheese, Red Pepper, and Cassis Relish

Grand Cayman

Using turkey instead of beef for burgers makes great nutritional sense as it is much lower in fat.

1 pound ground turkey meat
2 tablespoons fresh chopped parsley
1/4 cup minced onion
1/4 cup grated carrot
1 clove garlic, crushed
1/4 teaspoon cinnamon
1/4 teaspoon allspice
1/4 cup plain breadcrumbs
2/3 cup crumbled blue cheese
Red Pepper and Cassis Relish
4 English muffins, split and toasted
red onion slices

In a large bowl, combine all the ingredients except the blue cheese, relish, red onion, and muffins.

Preheat and lightly grease a barbecue grill. Form the meat into four patties and grill until cooked in the center. Sprinkle with blue cheese and allow to melt.

Serve on the English muffins with onion slices and Red Pepper and Cassis Relish.

YIELD: 4 SERVINGS

Rum Grilled Chicken and Roasted Red Pepper Sandwich
Dominica

The addition of melted mozzarella and basil to the red peppers makes a delightful combination.

4 tablespoons olive oil
juice of one lime
1 garlic clove, minced
1/2 cup gold or dark rum
1 large red bell pepper
2 skinless, boneless chicken breasts
2 slices of soft Mozzarella cheese
4 slices thick crusty French bread
1/4 cup fresh basil leaves
freshly ground pepper

In a small bowl stir together the olive oil, lime juice and garlic. In a separate container reserve 2 tablespoons and set aside. To the remaining mixture, add the rum.

Cut the bell pepper in quarters, lightly brush with the rum and olive oil mixture. Grill until slightly charred. Remove from heat and allow cooling. Peel the skin off the peppers and set aside.

On a wooden cutting board, pound the chicken breasts flat to about 1/2 inch. Brush with rum and oil mixture and marinate for 1 hour in the refrigerator. Grill chicken approximately 5 minutes per side until cooked through. Melt the mozzarella over the chicken.

Take the reserved oil, garlic and lime juice and brush the bread. Toast on the grill.

Place the chicken halves on the bread and arrange peppers and basil over this, topping with the remaining bread slice. Salt and pepper to taste.

Yield: 2 sandwiches

Roasting Peppers 101

For some mysterious reason, roasted peppers taste entirely different from raw or even sautéed peppers. Their flavors intensify and the difference is similar between that of a restaurant water glass and a piece of crystal.

*Cut bell peppers in half lengthwise, remove, and discard fibers and seeds.

*Place pepper hollow down on a lightly oiled (olive oil) baking sheet and flatten.

*Broil for several minutes until slightly charred.

*Remove from heat and allow to cool.

*The skins will readily slide off, discard them.

*Store in plastic zip top bags in refrigerator for up to 1 week.

Chutneys, Relishes and Dips

Looking for a little excitement to add to your meals or sandwiches? The addition of a fresh, homemade chutney, salsa or relish can make the simplest dish divine. Many of the following recipes are low in fat and will add spice and piquancy to grilled meats, fish and seafood.

CHUTNEYS are generally cooked, sweet and made with a fruit base. RELISHES are generally thicker than a salsa, have a crunchier texture and may be vegetable based. When making a SALSA use the freshest ingredients that you can find. Salsas can be hot, sweet and cooling all at once.

Avoid overcooking chutneys and relishes, as they tend to turn brown. The burnt sugar will impart a caramel flavor.

Containers for these luscious condiments vary from traditional sterilized canning jars with the rubber rings to recycled glass food jars. There are many unique shapes available now in canning jars, which are ideal for gift giving.

Most chutneys and relishes that are cooked will keep at room temperature for up to a year if hot-water processed. For safety's sake, I prefer to implement this procedure and refrigerate.

To hot-water process, fill sterilized jars with the chutney and follow the manufacturer directions for sealing. Lay an old dish towel on the bottom of a large deep stock pot, placing filled jars on top of it. Fill with water, covering the top of the jars by two inches of water. Bring to a boil for ten minutes. Remove jars with tongs and allow to cool.

Experiment and enjoy the following colorful recipes. Most are quick and easy to make and will add exuberance to appetizers, curries, chicken, meats, seafood and sandwiches.

Starfruit-Walnut Chutney

Dominica

Select star fruits that are an even yellow color, avoiding those with brown spots.

4 cups fresh, sliced star fruit
1 red onion, minced
1 red bell pepper, chopped
1/2 to 1 scotch bonnet, seeded and minced
1/2 teaspoon crushed garlic
1 teaspoon allspice
1/2 teaspoon cinnamon
2 tablespoons butter
2/3 cup apple cider vinegar
1 cup granulated sugar
1/2 cup walnuts, finely chopped
1/4 cup pear brandy or schnapps

In a large saucepan, sauté the starfruit, onions, peppers, garlic and the spices in the butter.

To the onions, add the vinegar and sugar, cooking over medium heat until thickened. Remove from heat and allow to cool completely.

In a small skillet, toast the walnuts until they give off a delicious aroma.

Stir in the brandy and walnuts. Pour into sterilized jars.

Yield: about 3 cups

Cointreau Mango Chutney
Barbados

The aroma of this chutney is just delightful. Serve on grilled fish, chicken or meats.

1/2 cup golden raisins
1/2 cup Cointreau
1 tablespoon walnut oil
1 large onion, minced
1/3 cup fresh limejuice
1 cup white wine vinegar
3/4 cup granulated sugar
2 cups fresh cubed mango, slightly unripe
1/2 cup peeled and diced cucumber
2/3 cup cauliflower florets
1/2 teaspoon cinnamon
1/8 teaspoon ground cloves
1 teaspoon yellow mustard seed
1/2 teaspoon nutmeg
1/2 Serrano pepper, peeled and seeded

Soak the raisins in the Cointreau for 1 hour.

In a medium sauté pan heat the oil and cook the onion until soft.

In a separate large saucepan, heat the lime juice, vinegar and sugar to boiling and remove from heat. Add the mango, cucumber, oranges and cauliflower and allow to sit for 30 minutes. Add the spices and onion. Drain and add the raisons, reserving the Cointreau. Simmer for 20 minutes, adding the liqueur and Serrano pepper the last 5 minutes. Allow to cool for one hour. Pour into sterilized jars.

YIELD: approximately 3 cups

Hot Banana Chutney
Trinidad

This spicy chutney owes its origins to the East Indian indentured servants, imported after the abolition of slavery in the 19th century. Goes well with curried chicken salad sandwiches.

1/2 teaspoon coriander
1/2 teaspoon turmeric
1/2 teaspoon cumin
1/4 teaspoon cloves
1/4 teaspoon cinnamon
2 tablespoons vegetable oil
1 yellow onion, minced
1/2 teaspoon crushed garlic
1 tablespoon fresh grated ginger
1 sweet red pepper, seeded and minced
1 Serrano pepper, seeded and minced
1/2 cup white vinegar
1/4 cup water
1 firm, ripe pear, peeled, cored, and chopped
4 large slightly unripe bananas, peeled and cut in 1/2 inch slices
salt and pepper to taste

In a medium saucepan, dry roast the spices for a few minutes until the volatile oils are released and their aroma permeates the air. Add the oil, onion, garlic, ginger and peppers, sautéing until the onion is clear. Add the vinegar, water, and sugar and bring to a boil.

Lower the heat to a quick simmer and add the pear, cooking for fifteen minutes. Add the bananas, salt and pepper and cook for two to three minutes. Allow to cool and refrigerate.

Use within 48 hours.

Yield: approximately 3 cups

Honeydew and Olive Chutney
Mexico

Pistachios add a crunchy texture to this surprisingly good chutney. Spread this on lox and cream cheese bagels.

1 cup firm honeydew melon finely cubed
1/2 cup green olives, pitted and finely chopped
1/2 cup calamata olives, pitted and finely chopped
1 small stalk celery, minced
1 small red onion, minced
1 habanero pepper, seeded and minced
1 teaspoon crushed garlic
1 tablespoon orange zest
1/2 cup shelled pistachios
juice of 1 lime
3/4 cup champagne vinegar
1 tablespoon olive oil
1 teaspoon each coriander, cumin, and mustard
1/2 cup sugar

Combine all ingredients in a heavy saucepan except pistachios and bring to boil. Remove from heat and allow to sit for 30 minutes. Return to heat and allow to simmer for 20 minutes. Remove from heat and add nuts.

Cool and pour into sterilized jars. Refrigerate.

YIELD: approximately 3 cups

Pineapple-Hazelnut Chutney
St. Thomas, U.S. Virgin Islands

1 teaspoon curry powder
1 tablespoon vegetable oil
1/2 cup white onion, minced
1/2 cup green bell pepper, seeded and minced
3/4 cup white vinegar
1/4 cup water
1 cup granulated white sugar
2 cups fresh diced pineapple
1/2 cup golden raisins
1/2 cup crushed hazelnuts

Heat the curry powder in a frying pan until slightly darkened and an aroma is released. Sauté the onion and bell pepper in the oil until the onion is just clear.

Heat the vinegar, water and sugar in a deep pot, brining to a boil. Add the pineapple and raisins, bringing to a boil, then reduce to simmer for 15 minutes. Remove from heat and allow the fruit to absorb the sugar and vinegar.

Return to heat and simmer for 25 minutes, until thickened. Add hazelnuts for the last 10 minutes. Pour into sterilized jars, cool and refrigerate. Will keep several months in refrigerator.

Yield: approximately 3 cups

Chunky Kiwi Tomato Relish
Martinique

Try serving this sweet-spicy relish with batter-dipped fried fish or mix with two tablespoons mayonnaise and 2/3 cup of milk for a lively salad dressing.

1 teaspoon turmeric
1 teaspoon cumin
1/2 teaspoon cinnamon
1/2 teaspoon nutmeg
1/4 teaspoon cardamom
1 teaspoon black mustard seeds
1 tablespoon olive oil
1 teaspoon crushed garlic
3 tablespoons fresh grated ginger
3 tablespoons chopped jalapeno peppers
2 large red onion, chopped
1 cup rice vinegar
1/2 cup sugar
3/4 cup fresh pineapple, cubed
1 pound ripe tomatoes, coarsely chopped and drained
6 large firm kiwis, peeled and chopped
1/4 cup dark Caribbean rum
1/2 teaspoon salt

In a medium sauté pan, dry roast the turmeric, cumin, cinnamon, nutmeg, cardamom and black mustard seeds until the spices slightly darken and a wonderful aroma is emitted. Add the olive oil, garlic, ginger, jalapenos and onion. Cook until the onion is soft.

In a medium saucepan with a lid, heat the rice vinegar and the sugar to boiling. Remove from heat adding the onion mixture and the pineapple. Allow to sit for 1/2 hour in order for pineapple to soak up the spices.

Return to medium heat and simmer for 15 minutes. Gently stir in tomato and kiwi, cooking gently for 20 minutes. Mixture will have thickened. Stir in the rum and salt, pouring into sterilized jars.

Yield: approximately 2 1/2 to 3 cups relish

Island Speak: Yo a regular snake in the grass.
Translation: I can't trust you.

Corn and Red Onion Relish
Cozumel

This chili flavored relish is perfect for nachos, burritos or even stirred into mayonnaise and served on top of a tuna sandwich.

2 cups corn kernels, fresh or thawed frozen
1 large red onion, minced
1 sweet red bell pepper, minced
1/4 cup sliced jalapeno peppers
1 cup fresh ripe tomato, chopped
1 teaspoon minced garlic
1-tablespoon chili powder
1/3 cup sugar
1 cup cider vinegar
1/2 teaspoon oregano
1/2 teaspoon salt

Place all ingredients in heavy saucepot and bring to boil. Lower to a simmer and cook for 10 minutes until corn kernels are soft.

Remove from heat and cool. Pour into sterilized jars and refrigerate.

This relish does not keep long so use within the week.

YIELD: APPROXIMATELY 3 1/2 CUPS

Fiery Ginger Cucumber Relish

Miami

The fire of this relish is cooled by smooth creamy yogurt. Excellent with roast lamb, jerked meats, and curries.

2 cups yogurt
2 large cucumbers, peeled and chopped
1 small onion, minced
2 tablespoons fresh grated ginger
1 serrano pepper, seeded and minced
2 cloves garlic, crushed
1/4 cup fresh mint leaves
juice of one lemon
1 teaspoon cracked black pepper
2 tablespoons olive oil

Place the yogurt into a colander lined with cheesecloth and allow to drain for two hours. Discard the whey. The cucumber must also be drained, so sprinkle lightly with salt and allow to drain in a colander.

In a large bowl, combine all other ingredients. Stir in the yogurt and cucumber and refrigerate.

Use by the next day.

YIELD: 2 CUPS

Caribbean Chow Chow
Tobago

Traditionally Chow Chow contains cauliflower and cabbage. The addition of green papaya adds a smooth bland taste, which combines well with the fiery habanero pepper. Serve with roast pork, hamburgers or as lunch condiment.

1 tablespoon olive oil
1/2 teaspoon cumin
1 teaspoon black mustard seeds
1 cup cauliflower florets
1 cup white cabbage, chopped
1/2 cup green papaya
1/2 cup peeled and chopped cucumber
1 small onion, chopped
1/2 habanero pepper, seeded and minced
1 clove garlic, crushed
3/4 cup rice vinegar
1/2 cup granulated sugar
2 teaspoons powdered mustard
1 teaspoon cracked black pepper
1/4 cup golden raisins

In medium sauce pan heat the oil and roast the mustard seeds and cumin until their aroma is released.

In a large saucepan, bring 2 quarts of water to a boil and blanch the cauliflower, papaya, and other vegetables for 1 minute. Drain in a colander.

In the medium saucepan with the spices, add the vinegar, sugar, and remaining spices and bring to a boil. Add the vegetables and raisins simmering for 5 minutes.

Remove from heat and cool. Will keep in the refrigerator for up to 10 days.

YIELD: 3 CUPS

Grand Marnier Onion and Orange Relish
Cuba

Serve this citrus-based relish with bagels and cream cheese for breakfast or as a compliment to salmon and new potatoes.

2 tablespoons olive oil
2 medium red onions, minced
1 clove garlic, crushed
1 Serrano pepper, seeded and minced
1 small red bell pepper, seeded and minced
4 large sweet oranges, peeled and chopped
1/4 cup fresh basil
1/2 teaspoon Chinese five spice powder
1/4 cup packed brown sugar
1 cup red wine vinegar
1/4 cup pimento-stuffed olives, chopped
2 tablespoons Grand Marnier
1/4 cup walnuts, crushed

In large saucepan, sauté the onions, garlic, and peppers in the olive oil until the onion is clear.

Add all remaining ingredients except the nuts and Grand Marnier; bring to a boil, and then simmer for 20 minutes. Remove from heat, add nuts, and allow to cool.

Stir in the Grand Marnier and pour into sterilized jars. If the hot water sterilization method is used this chutney will keep up to 6 months.

YIELD: 2 CUPS

Red Pepper and Cassis Relish
Nassau, Bahamas

This stunning dark red relish is made for roast chicken, turkey, or duck. Very nice with turkey and Jarlsberg sandwiches on whole grain bread.

6 sweet red bell peppers, finely chopped
1 large red onion, minced
1 lemon thinly sliced, chopped, peel and all
3/4 cup red wine vinegar
1/4 cup Crème de Cassis liqueur
1 cup sugar
1 teaspoon coriander seed
1/4 teaspoon cardamom
1/2 teaspoon salt
1 garlic clove crushed

Bring all ingredients to a boil in a large saucepan. Reduce heat and simmer until thickened.

Pour into sterilized jars and refrigerate. Keeps up to 2 months.

YIELD: 2 CUPS APPROXIMATELY

Island Speak: Night bring day. Translation: Things always seem better the next day.

Sesame Cabbage and Carrot Relish
Antigua

Serve this relish with roast pork or as a side salad/condiment at lunch.

3 tablespoons tahini paste
3 tablespoons rice vinegar
juice of one lemon
3 tablespoons brown sugar
1 tablespoon soy sauce
1 clove garlic, minced
1/2 teaspoon coriander
2 cups finely shredded white cabbage
2 cups finely shredded red cabbage
1 cup grated carrots
1/2 cup minced onion
1/2 cup raisins
1 tablespoon fresh grated ginger
1/2 teaspoon salt

Combine tahini, vinegar, lemon juice, sugar, soy sauce, garlic, and coriander.

In a large bowl, mix together cabbage, carrot, onion, raisins, ginger and salt. Pour tahini dressing over cabbage and toss well.

Serve the same day for best results.

YIELD: 4 TO 5 CUPS

Salsas are wonderful because they combine an array of flavors and are quick and simple to make. Some are fiery, some sweet, some sour, others are all of the above. For a truly different taste experience, try one of the following tropical-style recipes.

Pineapple Habanero Salsa

St. Croix

Serve this with grilled fish and a side of rice and black beans.

1 cup fresh finely cubed pineapple
1 sweet red bell pepper, chopped
1/2 cup minced red onion
1/2 habanero pepper, seeded and minced
1 teaspoon fresh zest of lime
juice of one lime
1 tablespoon apple cider vinegar
1 tablespoon olive oil
2 tablespoons fresh cilantro

Toss all ingredients together in a large bowl. Refrigerate for 1 hour before serving.

YIELD: 1 1/2 CUPS

Island Okra and Chayote Salsa
Barbados

I really like this with something sweet and crunchy such as coconut shrimp. This relish combines citrus, sweet and fire in one.

1 cup fresh finely sliced okra
1 cup chayote or zucchini, well chopped
1 medium yellow onion, minced
1 clove garlic, crushed
1/2 cup firm ripe mango, chopped
1 roasted red pepper, chopped
1 tablespoon capers
2 tablespoons fresh cilantro
1/2 habanero pepper minced
1 tablespoon honey
1 tablespoon champagne vinegar
juice of one lemon and one lime
2 tablespoons olive oil

In a large deep skillet, sauté the okra, chayote, onion and garlic for several minutes. Remove from heat and gently stir in other ingredients. Refrigerate overnight.

YIELD: Almost 3 cups

Did you know?: Chayote may be substituted with zucchini with excellent results. Also known as the Christophene, it is a type of squash that grows in sub-tropical and tropical climates. Quite similar to a pear in size and shape, the average chayote is about 4 to 5 inches long. The flesh ranges from pale, pale green to dark green and the pit may be eaten once cooked. Good source of potassium, as well as some vitamin C, folic acid, B6, and copper.

Purchasing: Select chayote with no marks and slightly firm.

Storage: Will keep up to several weeks in the refrigerator.

Preparation: Wear gloves while peeling the chayote as a sticky liquid comes out.

Sweet Potato and Citrus Salsa

St. John, U.S. Virgin Islands

This reminds me of the wonderful brunch served at Caneel Bay Plantation located in St. John, U. S. Virgin Islands. Serve with Virgin Island Meat Pie or jerked pork.

juice of one lemon and lime
2 tablespoons honey
2 tablespoons fresh cilantro
1 teaspoon red pepper flakes
1 teaspoon red hot pepper sauce
1 cup cooked, peeled and diced sweet potato
1 tablespoon orange zest
1 orange, peeled and diced
1/2 cup fresh diced pineapple
1 teaspoon fresh grated ginger

In a small bowl, mix the citrus juice, honey, cilantro, pepper flakes and hot sauce together until well combined.

In a large bowl, gently mix the remaining ingredients. Pour the citrus marinade over this and toss lightly. Refrigerate at least 2 hours.

YIELD: Approximately 2 cups

Tomato, Black Bean and Papaya Salsa
Puerto Rico

Use only ripe papaya for this Puerto Rican-inspired salsa. Goes well with fried plantains, rice and garlic shrimp.

2 tablespoons olive oil
juice of two lemons
3 tablespoons brown sugar
1 clove garlic minced
1 tablespoon apple cider vinegar
1 cup firm ripe papaya, peeled and cubed
1 cup ripe tomatoes, chopped
1 small red onion chopped
1/4 cup green olives, chopped
1/2 cup cooked black beans, drained

In a small bowl make a dressing of the following: oil, lemon juice, brown sugar, garlic and vinegar.

In a larger bowl, gently combine remainder of ingredients pouring dressing over the top and tossing.

Serve at room temperature. Refrigerate to store:

YIELD: APPROXIMATELY 3 CUPS

Island Speak: Love City Translation: St. John, U.S. Virgin Islands

Cha, Cha, Cha Corn Salsa

Puerto Rico

Nothing beats fresh salsa on corn chips. Instead of the regular yellow chips, try the blue corn chips available now. Look for the chip that combines sesame and blue corn as it is excellent.

1 cup corn kernels
1 cup fresh chopped tomatoes, drained
1/2 cup chopped yellow onion
1 small green bell pepper, minced
1 clove garlic crushed
2 jalapeno peppers, chopped
4 tablespoons cider vinegar
2 tablespoons olive oil
1 tablespoon brown sugar
1 tablespoon chili powder

In a large bowl, combine all ingredients well. Serve well chilled with corn chips, tacos or burritos.

YIELD: nearly 3 cups

Carnival Pepper and Walnut Salsa

St. Thomas

This good salsa receives its colors from four different colors of peppers. Serve with broiled swordfish or on tuna sandwiches with cheddar cheese.

2 tablespoons olive oil
1/2 teaspoon each: turmeric, cumin, and coriander
1 medium yellow onion, minced
1 clove garlic, crushed
1/2 cup cucumber, peeled and chopped
1 each: sweet red, orange, yellow and green bell pepper, seeded and diced
3 tablespoons chopped pimentos
4 tablespoons rice vinegar

Heat the spices in the olive oil until their aromatic oils are released. Do not over brown. Add onion, garlic, cucumber and peppers sautéing until onions are just clear and peppers still crunchy. Fold in pimentos

Remove from heat and cool for 20 minutes.

Stir in vinegar and combine well. Cool at least 3 hours in refrigerator.

YIELD: 2 TO 3 CUPS

Dips and Spreads

Dips and spreads are quite versatile in that they can be used for crunchy chips as well as healthful raw vegetables. Make out of the ordinary sandwiches to brighten a dreary afternoon. Dips need not be high in fat or calories. Use non-fat yogurt and tofu as a substitute for mayonnaise and cream cheese.

Piquant Chick-Pea Cumin Dip
Trinidad

Be sure to purchase the best quality and freshest spices available to impart top flavor.

1 tablespoon cumin seeds
1/4 teaspoon anise
12 ounces silken or soft tofu
1 garlic clove, crushed
3 tablespoons extra-virgin olive oil
2 cups cooked chick-peas
6 tablespoons sesame paste
juice of 1 lemon
1/2 teaspoon lemon zest
salt and freshly ground pepper to taste

In a small pan toast, the cumin seeds and anise until slightly browned and an aroma are released.

Using a food processor blend the tofu, garlic, oil, chick-peas, sesame paste, lemon juice and zest until smooth. Add in the spices and continue to blend. If a little too thick, add water by the tablespoon. Season with salt and pepper.

Serve with crisp fresh vegetables and whole grain flatbreads.

Yield: about 3 1/2 cups

Did you know?: Chickpeas or Garbanzo beans have been eaten for some 7,000 years, being very popular with the ancient Romans, Greeks, and Egyptians. Portuguese and Spanish explorers were successful in distributing the to the tropics. The beans vary in color from light beige, reddish brown, black and even green. Very good source of folic acid, potassium, magnesium, phosphorus, zinc, copper as well as numerous B vitamins and calcium.
Purchasing: May be purchased dried or canned.
Storing: Dried beans may be kept up until 1 year in a cool, dry place.
Preparation: Soak overnight and cook for 2 hours.

Mango Feta Dip with Walnuts
Grenada

Many of the recipes in this book rely on mangoes, from chicken dishes, salads, desserts and even spreads. Eating a mango is similar to a peach, only the flavor is magnified a 100 times. Don't be afraid to use this fragrant and adaptable fruit.

1 cup low-fat yogurt, drained
1/2 cup walnuts
1/2 cup cilantro leaves
1 cup ripe mango, finely diced
6 ounces feta cheese
1 teaspoon lime zest
1 tablespoon lime juice

Preheat oven to 350 degrees.

Toast the walnuts for about 5 or 6 minutes. Remove from oven and cool. Crush well.

Be sure to drain the yogurt well by placing in a colander for several hours. In a food processor, blend all the ingredients with the yogurt except the walnuts. Transfer to a serving bowl and fold in the nuts.

Serve as a sandwich with mixed greens, cucumbers and sprouts or with raw vegetables.

Yield: about 3 1/2 cups

Roasted Red Pepper and Coconut Spread
St. Martin, French West Indies

This is probably one of the more unusual combinations that I have come across in my travels and it really works. Make ahead and chill overnight for parties.

1 red bell pepper, quartered and seeded
1/2 cup freshly grated coconut
2 heads of garlic
1 small eggplant
1/4 cup plus 1 tablespoon extra-virgin olive oil
1/2 cup fresh parsley leaves

Roast the bell pepper, and coconut under the broiler until slightly charred. Remove, cool, and peel the skin, discarding it. Cut eggplant in 1/2 thick slices, brush with oil. Roast both the garlic and eggplant until tender. Test with a fork.

Squeeze pulp from the garlic and place with all other ingredients except coconut into a food processor.

Transfer to a bowl and fold in toasted coconut. Serve with flatbreads or garlic buttered toast points.

Yield: 1 1/2 cups

Peppery Tuna Habanero Dip

St. Thomas

No, this is not made with canned tuna fish. Use fresh for this classy bend on the traditional fish dip.

3/4 pound fresh tuna steak
1/2 cup plain yogurt
1/2 cup mayonnaise
1 stalk celery, finely diced
1/2 small yellow onion, minced
1 teaspoon freshly grated ginger
1 habanero pepper, seeded and minced
salt
freshly ground pepper to taste

Broil the tuna for 5 to 6 minutes on each side. Cool and chop well.

Blend all remaining ingredients in a food processor until smooth. Serve with toasted bagel chips.

Yield: 2 1/2 cups

Tomato Macadamia Spread
Bonaire

While on a long weekend on this lovely little island, this was served to me as a sandwich. It looked so appealing when the waiter served it, the couple next to me ordered the same thing. Use a nice dark bread such as pumpernickel and plenty of interesting greens, such as spinach, radicchio, mescalen and a sprinkling of sprouts.

1/2 cup crumbled feta cheese
1/2 cup ricotta cheese
1 tablespoon minced onion
3 tablespoons extra-virgin olive oil
2 tablespoons fresh parsley
1 teaspoon fresh oregano
1 tablespoon lime rum
1/2 teaspoon lime zest
1/4 cup macadamia nuts, chopped
1 medium ripe tomato, chopped

In a food processor, blend the cheeses, onion, olive oil, parsley, oregano, rum and lime zest.

Add the nuts, being careful not to over blend.

Fold in the tomatoes carefully.

Yield: 2 cups

Seasoning, Sauces and Condiments

The use of spices and sauces is integral to the nuances of Caribbean cooking. Not only are the taste buds delighted, but also stimulating flavors and dimension are added. Spices and produce from all over the world have found their way to the Caribbean.

First, we begin with the seasonings and sauces, which characterize Puerto Rican cuisine. Then on to the infamous jerk of Jamaica, the curries of Trinidad and the French islands, and the eye watering hot sauces indigenous to all the Caribbean islands. West Indian massalas, a version of curry, abound. Follow up these recipes with a generous spoonful of chutney.

Adobo

Puerto Rico

Adobo is a mix of ingredients rubbed into meat, fish, or poultry unique to Puerto Rico. Jarred or canned versions may be purchased in Hispanic supermarkets. Adobo also works well as a base for soups, sauces, and dips.

2 teaspoons pulverized sea or rock salt
1/2 teaspoon coarsely cracked black pepper
1/2 teaspoon ground cumin
1/2 teaspoon coriander
1/2 teaspoon ground ginger
1 teaspoon ground oregano
2 garlic cloves, chopped
1 teaspoon olive oil
1 teaspoon fresh lime juice

Combine all ingredients in a mortar and pestle, except the olive oil and lime juice. Use an up and down rubbing motion to grind the ingredients together. Slowly incorporate the oil and limejuice, combining well.

Yield: enough for recipe that serves 6 to 8

Sofrito

Puerto Rico

Sofrito means to 'cook slowly'. Even though sofrito may be stored for a couple of days in glass in the refrigerator, it is recommended to make a fresh batch for each use. Sofrito is used to flavor many mixed rice, vegetable, seafood, chicken, and meat dishes.

1/3 cup minced smoked ham
1/3 cup olive oil
6 garlic cloves, minced
1 small green bell pepper, seeded and minced
3 sweet chili peppers, seeded and minced
1 small onion, minced
2 teaspoons chopped fresh oregano
2 teaspoons chopped fresh cilantro
2 medium tomatoes, chopped
1 tablespoon tomato paste
salt and freshly ground pepper to taste

Sauté the ham, garlic, peppers, and onion in the olive oil for 3 minutes. Reduce heat and add remaining ingredients, cooking gently for 20 minutes.

Yield: about 1 1/2 cups

Aji-li-mojili Sauce

Puerto Rico

This very nice garlic and pepper sauce will enhance the flavor of many hot and cold dishes. It is also the base for other sauces. May be made ahead and refrigerated.

8 garlic cloves, peeled, and crushed
8 peppercorns
3 pimentos
1 hot chili pepper, seeded and minced
1/4 cup fresh lime juice
1/4 cup white vinegar
1/2 cup olive oil
2 teaspoons salt

In a large mortar and pestle, pulverize the garlic, peppercorns, and pimentos along with the hot chili pepper. Form a coarse paste; add the lime juice, vinegar, olive, and salt, using a spoon to mix.. The garlic sauce will retain a coarse texture.

Yield: 1 1/4 cups

Jerk Rub

Jamaica

This rub can be made as hot or mild as you like it. Substitute milder chili peppers for the habaneros. May be stored in the refrigerator for about 3 to 4 weeks.

1/2 cup minced scallions
1/2 cup minced yellow onion
2 garlic cloves, crushed
2 small habanero peppers, seeded and minced
2 teaspoons fresh thyme leaves
1 teaspoon allspice
1 teaspoon freshly ground black peppers
1 1/2 teaspoons salt
dash of ground nutmeg, ginger, and cinnamon

Use a mortar and pestle or a food processor to grind all ingredients into a paste. Refrigerate in a tightly closed glass jar. Excellent rubbed into meat, seafood, and chicken over a slow barbeque.

Colombo

Guadeloupe

Colombo derives its name from the city of Colombo in Sri Lanka. This French West Indian version of curry was introduced by migrant Hindu workers. Stores well in a glass jar. Heating the spices releases the volatile oils subtly changing and improving the flavor.

1/4 cup turmeric
1 teaspoon mustard seeds
1/2 teaspoon cloves
1/2 teaspoon cinnamon
1/4 cup cumin seeds
1/4 cup coriander seeds
1 tablespoon black peppercorns
1/2 teaspoon whole cloves

In a dry skillet over low to medium heat, toast the spices until a pleasant aroma is released—several minutes. Remove from heat, allowing cooling.

Grind spices in a peppermill and store in an airtight glass jar. Do not store in plastic as this will absorb the oils and distort the flavor.

Yield: approximately 3/4 cup

Curry powder
Trinidad

There is some question whether curry came to the islands via the British colonists or the indentured East Indians brought over to replace the newly freed African slaves. Commercial curry powder may be purchased at the local grocery; homemade is far superior.

1/2 cup coriander seeds
1/4 cup turmeric
2 tablespoons cumin seeds
1/2 teaspoon whole cloves
2 tablespoons whole black peppercorns
1/2 teaspoon cardamom
1 tablespoon ground ginger
1 tablespoons black mustard seeds
1 tablespoon broken cinnamon stick

In a heavy dry skillet over low to medium heat toast the ingredients until the mustard seeds begin to pop and an aroma is released—about three minutes. Remove from skillet and allow cooling.

Put through a spice mill or in the blender and grind finely. Store in a tightly closed glass container.

Yield: about 1 cup

Island Speak: Don't humbug me. Translation: Don't bother me.

Massala

Trinidad

This is another excellent substitute for curry. in a more paste-like form.

1 teaspoon saffron threads
1 teaspoon ground turmeric
1/4 cup coriander seeds
1 tablespoon black peppercorns
2 teaspoons cumin seeds
1 teaspoon fenugreek seeds
1/2 teaspoon whole cloves
1 teaspoon black mustard seeds
1 large onion, minced
3 garlic cloves, chopped
1 habanero pepper, seeded and minced

In a large heavy skillet, toast the spices for three minutes until fragrant. Remove from heat to cool.

Run spices through the spice mill until finely ground. In a food processor, puree the onion, garlic, and habanero until smooth. Add in spices and combine into a paste. Use at once or the next day.

Yield: about 1 cup

Creole Sauce

St. Martin

This sauce can be used with meat, fish, or chicken.

1 large onion, minced
1/4 cup olive oil
1 red bell pepper, seeded and finely chopped
1/2 cup vegetable or chicken stock
1/2 cup white wine
juice of one lime
1/2 teaspoon lime zest
2 medium tomatoes, diced
1 tablespoon tomato paste
1/2 small fiery chili
1 bay leaf
1/4 teaspoon ground cloves
1/2 teaspoon grated nutmeg
1/4 teaspoon ground mace
salt and freshly ground pepper to taste

In a saucepan, sauté the onion and peppers in the oil for three minutes. Add the stock, wine, vinegar and lime juice and zest. Stir in tomatoes, tomato paste, fiery chili, bay leaf and spices. Simmer for until thickened. Season with salt and pepper to taste. Remove bay leaf.

Yield: nearly 2 cups

Native Seasoning
The Virgin Islands

Also known as Creole seasoning, this spice mixture can be successfully stored in an airtight glass jar in the refrigerator and will enhance fish, poultry or meat.

1 cup pulverized rock salt
1 tablespoon freshly ground pepper
4 garlic cloves, peeled, and crushed
1 stalk celery, finely minced
1 tablespoon fresh parsley, chopped
2 tablespoons pimento-stuffed olives, finely diced
1 medium onion, minced
1 fresh hot chili pepper, seeded and minced
juice of one lime
1 tablespoon vinegar

Either in a mortar and pestle or in the blender, combine all ingredients until a smooth paste is formed. Store only in a glass jar in a refrigerated place. Keeps for up to a week.

Yield: approximately 2 cups

Habanero sauce

Martinique

*A*lways be sure to handle these peppers or any other hot chili peppers with care. Gloves are suggested since on more than one occasion have I stuck a finger near my eye with painful results. .

1/4 olive oil
6 large scotch bonnet peppers, seeded, and minced
1 large yellow onion, minced
2 garlic cloves, minced
1/4 water
1 cup malt vinegar
1 teaspoon salt
1 teaspoon freshly ground black pepper

In a saucepan, heat the oil and sauté the peppers, onion, and garlic until the onion is soft but not brown. Add the water and simmer another 15 minutes. Remove from heat and stir in the vinegar, salt, and pepper.

Place in sterilized glass jars. Use within one month.

Yield: approximately 2 cups

Did you know? Chile peppers were first used for ornamental purposes? Chili or hot peppers are members of the nightshade family, including eggplants, tomatoes, and potatoes. Originating in South and Central America, there are about 10 species of hot peppers, all of which have different, size, shape, color, and taste. Some are relatively mild and others scorching hot.

Heat Guide

Anaheim, Ancho, Poblano, Pasillas . . . . .mild

Jalapeno, Cascabels, Chipolte . . . . .lively

De Arbol, Hungarian Hot Wax Pepper, Serrano . . . . fiery

Cayenne, Pequins, Fresno, Thai .meltdown

Habanero, a.k.a. Scotch Bonnet . . . . .nuclear blast!

Purchasing: Chile peppers may be purchased fresh or dried. For fresh, choose peppers with a glossy, firm skin, with no soft spots. Dried peppers are acceptably wrinkled.

Storing: Keep fresh peppers in the vegetable compartment in the refrigerator for approximately one week. Dry peppers should be kept in an airtight container in a cool dark place for 3 to 4 months.

Preparation: When handling hot peppers, take care to wear gloves and protect eyes. Keep hands away from face and skin. To season, start with small amounts added to recipes. It is always easier to add more than try and dilute an inedible dish.

Hot mango chili ketchup

St. Croix, U.S. Virgin Islands

Use slightly under ripe mangos in this luscious sauce. Good on coconut shrimp, jerked dishes, and rice-combinations.

1 teaspoon cumin
1 teaspoon turmeric
1/4 cup olive oil
1 large onion, minced
2 cloves garlic, minced
6 hot chili peppers, seeded and minced
1 cup malt vinegar
1/3 cup granulated white sugar
2 cups mango, diced
1 teaspoon salt

In a dry sauce pan, toast the cumin and turmeric until fragrant—about two to three minutes. In the same pan, add the oil and sauté the onion, garlic, and peppers until onions are just soft.

Add vinegar, sugar, mango, and salt simmering for 15 minutes. Remove from heat and allow to cool. Pour into a blender or food processor and puree until smooth. Place into sterilized jars and refrigerate. Use within four weeks.

Yield: approximately 3 cups

Did you know? Curry is not one spice, yet a blend of as few as 5 spices and up to 50 ingredients. The basic spices are cinnamon, turmeric, coriander, cumin, pepper, cardamom, ginger, nutmeg, and cloves. Depending on geographic location, also included can be caraway, anise, fennel, fenugreek, mustard seeds, and saffron. Curry can be hot or mild.
Purchasing: Curry can come pre-mixed or better yet purchase fresh spices and grind your own as needed.
Storage: Never store spices in plastic as this will absorb the volatile oils and quickly spoil the flavor. Store in glass where it is cool and dry.
Preparation: Toast the spices until slightly darkened and an aromatic flavor is released just before adding to a recipe.

Curried papaya butter
Cayman Islands

Poured into pretty glass bottles and tied with raffia or ribbon, this makes a wonderful hostess gift. Serve with lobster, crab, chicken, or fish.

2 cups ripe papaya, diced
1 tablespoon papaya seeds
juice of one lime
1/2 teaspoon lime zest
2 tablespoons malt vinegar
1 tablespoon cream of coconut
1/2 teaspoon cumin
2 teaspoons curry powder

Puree all ingredients in the blender. The papaya seeds will add a nice spicy kick.

In a double boiler, cook until slightly thickened. Place in sterilized jars after cooling. Will keep up to two weeks in the refrigerator.

Yield: approximately 2 cups

Pineapple-passion fruit mayonnaise
Dominican Republic

Use as a salad dressing on chicken or seafood salads. Also works well on fish fillet and chicken sandwhiches.

1 cup good mayonnaise
1/4 cup pineapple, diced
1/4 cup fresh passionfruit, peeled and seeded
1/4 teaspoon cumin
1/2 teaspoon freshly cracked black pepper

Puree all ingredients in the blender. Use within two days.

Yield: 1 1/2 cups

Avocado-banana salad dressing
Aruba

Very nice on roasted vegetable or seafood salads and low in calories as well.

2 large avocados, peeled, pitted and diced
1 medium banana, cut in chunks
1 garlic clove, crushed
1 cup plain, non or low-fat yogurt
juice of one lime
grating of lime zest
1 tablespoon freshly cracked black pepper
1/2 teaspoon cumin
1/2 teaspoon turmeric
grating of ginger and cinnamon
dash of fiery hot sauce

Puree all ingredients in the food processor or blender. Chill for several hours and use at once.

Yield: about 2 1/2 cups

Island Speak: Wha don meet yo, don pass yo. Translation: Don't worry about things that haven't happened yet.

Guava-macadamia barbeque sauce
Cuba

Guava is an evergreen tree that attains up to 30 feet in height. At a mere 18 months of age, it will begin to bear for the next 40 years. Guavas bruise easily when ripe, so select green ones and keep in the refrigerator until ready to use. When ready, remove and they will ripen after several days at room temperature.

6 ripe guavas
1/2 cup minced onion
2 tablespoons olive oil
1/2 cup macadamia pieces, toasted
1 tablespoon freshly grated ginger
1 teaspoon hot chili sauce
1 teaspoon salt
1/4 cup tomato paste

To make guava paste, cut fruit in half and mash shells and all. Force through a sieve to remove seeds, reserving both the pulp and shells. Puree pulp and shells and set aside.

Sauté the onion until clear in the olive oil. Cool. Pour onions and oil into a blender along with remaining ingredients. Refrigerate overnight to bring out full flavor. Mixture will be slightly chunky from the nuts.

More sides
and
Vegetables

No Caribbean meal would be complete without its compliment of side dishes. In this chapter, we will explore the traditional ranging from fried plantain, fungi, pigeon peas, and rice to nouvelle Caribbean cuisine such as Orange-Coconut Rice, Banana Curried Cauliflower and Lemon-Saffron Black Beans.

St. Thomas Fungi

The Virgin Islands

Recalling the first time that fungi was encountered, I remember just staring at it to figure out what it was. Since then, many variations of this island staple have been come by; this one is my personal favorite.

1 tablespoon vegetable oil for frying
1/4 cup minced yellow onion
1/2 cup diced okra
2 1/2 cups boiling water
1 1/4 cups yellow cornmeal
1 teaspoon salt
1 teaspoon freshly grated black pepper

Sauté the onion in the oil until soft. Remove from heat.

Boil the okra for several minutes in the water. Keep the water at a full boil and add in the cornmeal and other ingredients. Keep stirring to remove all lumps. Reduce heat, cover, and cook for an additional 5 minutes. Serve at once.

Yield: 4 servings

Fried plantains
St. Croix, U.S. Virgin Islands

Plantains comes from the banana family, but must be cooked. Select firm plantains with plenty of dark brown spots to indicate ripeness.

2 large ripe plantains, slices in 1/2 inch slices diagonally
vegetable oil for frying
paper towels

Soak the plantain slices in salted water for 5 minutes. Remove and pat dry.

Heat the oil in a deep skillet and fry the plantain slices until golden. Drain on paper towels and serve at once.

Yield: 4 servings

Pigeon peas and rice

Puerto Rico

Pigeon peas may also be purchased canned from ethnic groceries. Serve with Creole fish dishes and jerked or barbequed foods.

2 tablespoons olive oil
1 small yellow onion, minced
1 stalk celery, minced
1 clove garlic, crushed
1/2 green bell pepper, seeded, and minced
2 cups shelled pigeon peas
1 tablespoon tomato paste
1/4 teaspoon cumin
1/2 teaspoon thyme
4 cups water
2 cups white rice
salt and pepper to taste

In a deep saucepan, sauté the onion, celery, pepper, and garlic in the oil until onion is soft. Remove from pan and set aside. Add water to saucepan and bring to boil. Boil peas until just barely tender. Return vegetables to pan along with tomato paste and spices.

Add rice and bring to boil. Reduce heat and cook until all water is absorbed.

Yield: eight servings

Piquant Chayote Coconut Gratin
Guadeloupe

*A*lso known as Christophene, this is the fruit of an edible plant native to Central America and Mexico—a type of squash that proliferates in tropical climates—originating with the Aztecs and Mayans. Choose unblemished fruit, which is slightly firm.

4 medium chayotes
1 medium onion, minced
3 scallions, chopped
1 small habanero pepper, seeded and minced
1 clove garlic, minced
2 tablespoons olive oil
1/4 cup coconut milk
1/4 cup graham crackers, crushed
1 cup shredded aged, extra-sharp white cheddar cheese

Place the chayotes in a large saucepan of salted water and boil until just slightly soft, about 20 minutes. Remove from heat and cool.

Slice fruit in half and scoop out the pulp and reserve, leaving shells intact.

Sauté the onions, scallions, peppers, and garlic in the olive oil. Mash along with the chayote pulp and the coconut milk.

Preheat oven to 350∞.

Fill the chayote shells with the pulp mixture and top first with graham cracker crumbs and cheddar. Place in a glass baking dish and bake for 15 minutes or until delicately browned.

Yield: 4 servings

Lemon-saffron black beans

Puerto Rico

This is yet another version of the traditional Caribbean black beans. Serve with white rice.

6 saffron threads
4 cups hot water
2 cups black beans
3 tablespoons olive oil
1 large yellow onion, minced
3 garlic cloves, minced
1 fiery chili pepper, seeded and minced
juice of one lemon
1 teaspoon fresh lemon zest
1/2 teaspoon dried crushed oregano
1 bay leaf
1 tablespoon sugar
3 tablespoon cider vinegar
salt and pepper to taste

Soak the saffron in the hot water for 15 minutes. Meanwhile, cover the beans with cold water, rinse, and drain. Repeat and thoroughly remove dust and small sticks and stones from beans. Cover beans with water in a deep pot, bring to boil, remove from heat and let sit for one hour. Drain the beans and now cover with the saffron infused water. Bring to a full rolling boil, reduce heat, and simmer.

In a small saucepan, heat the oil and sauté the onion, garlic, and chili pepper until the onion is soft. Add this to the beans along with the lemon, lemon zest, oregano, bay leaf, and sugar. Cover pot tightly and simmer for 45 minutes.

Add vinegar and continue to simmer for 30 minutes. Season with salt and pepper.

Yield: 6 to 8 servings

Island Speak: Watch out fo da cowfoot woman. Translation: This legend is found with some variation on nearly every Caribbean island. Mystical jumbi or spirit living in the bush that steals children.

Coconut Tutu

St. Martin, Netherland Antilles

This cornmeal mush with black-eyed peas is a souped-up version of fungi.

1 cup black-eyed beans, soaked overnight in cold water
2 cups water
2 cups unsweetened coconut milk
1 cup yellow cornmeal
1 small onion, minced
1 garlic clove, minced
2 tablespoons olive oil
1 1/2 teaspoon salt
1/4 cup lightly packed brown sugar
2 tablespoon freshly chopped parsley
unsweetened grated coconut

Rinse and drain the peas. Heat the water and coconut milk to boiling and add the peas. Bring to boil again, reduce heat, and simmer until peas are tender. Gradually stir in corn meal, stirring briskly to avoid lumps. Cook for 5 additional minutes over low heat.

Sauté the onion and garlic until soft in the oil. Stir into the cornmeal mixture along with the salt and brown sugar.. Use an ice cream scoop to serve out portions. Sprinkle with grated coconut and parsley.

Yield: 6 to 8 servings

Hot lulu

Cayman Islands

I had never heard of this dish until visiting Grand Cayman, so it must be unique to those islands—it is fabulous with the addition of hot sauce.

1 cup grated apple
1 cup grated carrot
1 cup grated sweet potato
1/2 cup minced onion
1 tablespoon olive oil
1 cup all-purpose flour
1/2 cup packed brown sugar
3/4 cup butter
1 tablespoon habanero hot sauce
1/2 teaspoon salt
1/2 teaspoon cinnamon
4 tablespoons brown sugar

Preheat oven to 350∞.

Combine all ingredients well except the 4 tablespoons of brown sugar and pour into a buttered casserole dish. Bake covered for 45 minutes.

Remove cover and sprinkle the 4 tablespoons of brown sugar over the top. Return to oven and broil until sugar is bubbly. Serve at once as a side dish to any main course. Makes a nice foil to spicy dishes.

Yield: 6 servings

Green Bean and mashed plantain loaf

Dominican Republic

Very rich and filling.

4 large ripe plantains, peeled and cut in chunks
6 cups of salted hot water
1 medium onion, minced
1 tablespoon olive oil
1 tablespoon butter
2 eggs, beaten
1 tablespoon flavored rum such as coconut or banana
2 cups cooked green beans (slightly under-cook) cut up
1/2 cup breadcrumbs
1/2 teaspoon nutmeg
1/2 teaspoon salt
1/2 cup grated parmesan cheese

Boil the plantains in the salted water for about 20 minutes. Remove from heat and drain. Sauté the onion in the olive oil until soft and remove from heat.

Preheat oven to 350∞. Mash the plantains along with the butter, eggs, and flavored rum. Grease a glass baking dish with butter and place half of the ripe plantain mixture in the bottom.

Next, layer the onions with the green beans and top with remaining plantain mixture. In a small bowl, combine the breadcrumbs nutmeg, salt, and cheese. Sprinkle this over the top.

Cover and bake for 15 minutes, remove cover and bake an additional 5 minutes.

Yield: 6 servings

Mofongo
Puerto Rico

Mofongo can be found on nearly every Puerto Rican menu, whether in the metropolis of San Juan or out in the country.

3 large green plantains, peeled and sliced diagonally in 1/2 " slices
oil for frying
1/2 cup fried pork skin, broken in small pieces
1 garlic clove
1 teaspoon salt

Fry the plantains in the oil, until barely golden. Mash the plantain along with the remaining ingredients and form into balls. Serve hot.

Yield: 6 servings

Orange-banana sweet potatoes

St. Thomas, U.S. Virgin Islands

Make this sophisticated side dish ahead of time.

3 sweet potatoes, peeled and diced
5 large oranges
2 large ripe bananas
1/2 cup brown sugar
1/2 cup melted butter
1/2 teaspoon freshly grated ginger

In a large pot, boil the sweet potato until tender, about 30 minutes. Remove from heat, drain, and cool.

Cut the tops from four of the oranges and carefully scoop out the pulp. Squeeze the juice and grate the rind from the fifth orange.

Preheat oven to 350∞.

Reserve 2 tablespoons of the orange zest and mash all other ingredients together until smooth. Fill the orange shells and bake for 15 minutes. Remove from oven and sprinkle with orange zest.

Yield: 4 servings

Spicy Dal
Trinidad

Serve with plenty of hot rice either alone or with meat or chicken dishes.

2 cups lentils
1/2 teaspoon curry powder
1/2 teaspoon turmeric
1/2 teaspoon cumin
4 cups water
2 tablespoons ghee (clarified butter) or vegetable oil
1 medium onion, minced
1/2 small habanero pepper, seeded and minced
1 teaspoon black mustard seeds
1/2 teaspoon cracked black pepper
1 teaspoon salt

Soak the lentils in cold water overnight. Drain and rinse the following day. Heat the spices in a deep saucepan until fragrant, about 3 minutes. Add the water and lentils, simmer over low heat.

Meanwhile, heat the ghee in a small sauté pan and cook the onion, habanero, mustard seeds, and black pepper until the seeds pop. Add to the lentils along with salt. Simmer until tender.

Serve hot over rice with chutney.

Yield: 6 servings

Island Speak: Yo well batty Translation: You're crazy

Orange Coconut Rice

British Virgin Islands

Traditionally British food has been considered bland at best. It certainly has come a long way in the Caribbean.

1/2 cup minced onion
1 garlic clove minced
1 teaspoon fresh thyme, chopped
1 tablespoon olive oil
1 large orange, peeled, sectioned and seeded
1 tablespoon orange zest
1/2 cup unsweetened coconut flakes
2 cups hot cooked white rice
2 tablespoons fresh parsley chopped
salt and pepper to taste

Sauté the onion, garlic, and thyme in the olive oil until the onion is clear. Chop the orange sections into small pieces.

Toss all remaining ingredients together and serve hot, at once.

Yield: 4 servings

Banana Curried Cauliflower

Bermuda

Goes well with hot and spicy dishes served with white rice and chutney.

2 teaspoon curry powder
1 tablespoon vegetable oil
1 medium onion
1 medium apple
1/2 cup water
1/2 cup coconut milk
1 teaspoon salt
1 1/2 cups lightly steamed cauliflower florets
1 tablespoon dark rum
1/4 cup raisins
3 slightly green bananas, peeled, and sliced
1/2 teaspoon lime zest

In a dry, large frying pan, toast the curry powder until fragrant for about 3 minutes. In the same pan, sauté the onions until soft in the oil.

Add the apple and cook over low heat for 3 or 4 minutes. Pour in water, coconut milk, salt, cauliflower, rum, and raisins, and cook until slightly thickened. Add bananas and continue over low heat for 5 minutes.

Remove from heat and serve at once.

Yield: 4 servings

Green tomatoes and okra

Nassau, Bahamas

May be served as a side dish or over rice.

2 tablespoons sesame oil
1 clove garlic minced
1/2 cup minced yellow onion
2 large green tomatoes, diced
1 cup fresh diced okra
1 teaspoon vinegar
1 teaspoon lime juice
1/2 teaspoon salt
1 teaspoon sugar
dash of hot chili pepper sauce
sesame seeds, toasted

Sauté the onion and garlic in the oil until the onion is soft. Add the tomatoes and okra, cook over medium heat for 5 minutes. Add the vinegar, lime juice, sugar, salt and hot chili pepper sauce. Cook until thickened.

Serve at once and garnish with toasted sesame seeds.

Yield: 4 servings

Did you know? Okra belongs to the same family as the hibiscus and cotton plant? Brought to the United States by African slaves, okra grows in warm climates. Good source of potassium, magnesium, and folic acid.
Purchasing: Buy okra that is 2 to 4 inches in length, as it will still be young and tender. Do not buy if sticky, as it will be over ripe.
Storing: Okra spoils quickly, so store in the refrigerator wrapped in paper towel or a paper bag for a couple of days. To freeze, blanch with water for 1 minute.

How Sweet It Is

I am one of those people that checks out the dessert menu first. The ideal dinner to me would be appetizer, salad, and desert. O.K. we all know that we need protein, carbohydrate, and water to survive. Personally, I need dessert to survive. This is my emotional crutch. Is this bad for me? I don't think so. Everything in moderation—after all, you only live once.

Frozen Banana-Mango Mousse

St. Barthelemy

For a different and exotic ending to a dinner party, try this divine mouse. Quick and easy to make as well.

3 bananas
2 mangos
salt
1/4 cup sugar
1/2 cup water
1 teaspoon unflavored gelatin
1 pint heavy cream, whipped

Put bananas and mango in food processor or blender adding a few grains of salt.

In a small saucepan, bring water to boil, adding sugar and gelatin until dissolved. Add to fruit mixture, stirring well. Put in large glass bowl and refrigerate until thick. Remove from refrigerator and beat with an electric beater until fluffy.

Fold in whipped cream and spoon in to freezer trays, a mold, or ice-cube trays.

Yield: 4 servings

Island Speak: jumbi wak Translation: Jumbi is a spirit, hence the spirit walks, i.e. I hear an unexplained noise in the bush.

Frozen Pina Colada Pie

St. Lucia

This pie is a lively finale to any summertime party.

1 store-bought baked piecrust
1/3 cup Coco Lopez (sweetened cream of coconut)
1/3 cup frozen pineapple juice concentrate
2 ounces 151 proof rum
1/2 cup whipped topping
1 1/2 cups vanilla ice cream

In a small bowl, combine the cream of coconut, pineapple juice, rum, and whipped topping. Put ice cream in a large heavy bowl, and quickly mash and stir in the coconut mix. The alcohol will soften the ice cream a bit and make it easier to work with.

Spoon into the piecrust and freeze several hours until firm.

Cut in pie-like wedges to serve.

PS You can add more rum if you want to!

Yield: 6 to 8 servings

Banana Daiquiri Cheesecake
St. Thomas, U.S. Virgin Islands

St. Thomas is famous for its banana daiquiris. Everyone claims to have the original recipe. For those of us with a penchant for cheesecake, here is my tribute.

1 1/2 cups crushed vanilla wafers
1/4 cup crushed almonds
1/4 cup granulated sugar
1/4 cup melted butter
2 8-ounce packages cream cheese, cut up
2 tablespoons all-purpose flour
1 8 ounce carton sour cream
1/3 cup granulated sugar
2 eggs
1 egg yolk
1 package banana pudding mix
2 medium bananas, mashed
1 teaspoon fresh zest of lemon
1/2 teaspoon vanilla
1/2 teaspoon rum extract
1 teaspoon baking powder

Combine crushed vanilla wafers, almonds, 1/4 cup sugar and melted butter in small bowl. Press into bottom and up a couple of inches into a standard 8 or 9-inch spring-form pan.

In a large mixer bowl, combine cream cheese, flour, sour cream, and 1/3 cup sugar. Mix in eggs, pudding mix, and all other ingredients until just smooth.

Pour into crust and bake at 350 degrees for 30 to 40 minutes.

Yield: 6 to 8 servings

TIP: How do you know if the cheesecake is done? —when the center appears set but moves when you shake the pan.

Did you know? Bananas belong to the orchid and lily family? Believed to be close to one million years old, its origins appear to be Malaysia. Bananas grow in sub-tropical and tropical climates reaching up to 26 feet in height. Plants attain maturity quickly, bearing fruit after one year.

Purchasing: Ripe bananas are bright yellow in color with a few brown spots.

Storing: Store ripe bananas in a cool, dry place. Do not refrigerate as the skins will turn black. Bananas will keep in the freezer for up to 2 months. Puree and add lime or lemon juice to avoid oxidation and an unattractive dark cast.

Preparation: Do not peel the fruit, until immediately ready to use as it will discolor and become mushy.

The Best Key Lime Pie

St. Thomas, U.S. Virgin Islands

Having tried many different methods including baking and not baking the pie, this one had the best thick and creamy texture and the most intense flavor.

Filling:
Juice of 5 limes
3 teaspoons grated lime zest
5 large egg yolks, or 6 small ones
1 14-ounce can, plus an additional 1/4 cup sweetened condensed milk

crust:
1 1/2 cups finely crushed graham crackers
3 tablespoons granulated sugar
1 tablespoon brown sugar
6 tablespoons butter at room temperature
1 teaspoon almond extract

topping:
1 cup heavy cream
1/4 cup, plus 1 tablespoon confectioner's sugar

Put yolks in a large bowl and whisk in zest, until frothy—about 2 to 3 minutes. Slowly stir in milk and then lime juice.. Put aside.

Preheat oven to 325∞. In a smaller bowl, mix the graham crackers with the sugars. Cut in softened butter with 2 knives or a fork, sprinkling in almond extract. Combine well. Press into the bottom of a 9-inch pie pan—glass works best. Bake for 12 minutes, removing from oven.

Pour the filling into the pie shell. Bake at 350°for approximately 15 minutes. Remove from oven and when sufficiently cooled, refrigerate until thoroughly chilled, 3 to 4 hours.

Whip the cream and slowly stir in the sugar by spoonfuls. Cream should form peaks. Serve pie with large dollops of whipped cream.

Yield: 8 servings

Sweet Potato and Pineapple Pie with Macadamia Crust

Puerto Rico

This unlikely pie is just wonderful and good for you too. I have served this at elegant dinner parties as well as on-the-beach picnics.

Preheat oven to 350 degrees.

1/4 cup whole wheat flour
1/2 cup all-purpose flour
1/2 cup cornmeal
1/2 teaspoon ground pepper
1 tablespoon brown sugar
1/2 cup butter, cut up
cold water
1/2 teaspoon lemon extract
1/2 cup crushed macadamia nuts
1/4 teaspoon cinnamon
1/4 cup butter
2 tablespoons honey
2 cups diced and cooked sweet potatoes
1 cup sour cream
2 tablespoons flour
4 eggs, beaten
1 egg yolk
1/4 teaspoon allspice
1 teaspoon cinnamon
1/2 teaspoon fresh grated ginger
1 teaspoon fresh zest of lemon
1 teaspoon fresh zest of orange
1/2 cup well-packed brown sugar
1 teaspoon vanilla
1/2 teaspoon salt
whipped cream or vanilla ice-cream for topping

Prepare cornmeal pastry by sifting together 1/4 cup whole-wheat flour, corn-meal, and 1/2 cup all-purpose flour, ground pepper and 1-tablespoon brown sugar. Cut in the 1/2 cup butter with a fork or two knives until crumbly. Add a little cold water and the lemon extract to form into a ball. Roll out and press into a pie tin. In a small bowl, mix the crushed nuts, 1/4 teaspoon cinnamon, 1/4 cup butter, and the honey. Spread this in the bottom of the crust.

In a very large bowl, mash the sweet potatoes with the sour cream, flour, egg yolk, and beaten eggs. Stir in the remaining spices, ginger, lemon, and orange zest, 1/2 cup brown sugar, vanilla, and salt. Fold in the pineapple.

Spoon this into the pastry crust.

Bake at 350 degrees for 25 minutes until a toothpick comes out clean.

Serve with whipped cream or vanilla ice cream.

Yield: 6 to 8 servings

Island Speak: Allyuh Translation: All of you people

Chocolate Orange Curacao Cake
St. Croix, U.S. Virgin Islands

As a child, my European mother would flavor the frosting for chocolate cakes with orange essence, resulting in the most delectable flavor. As we read earlier, Europe and the Caribbean when first introduced, exchanged and substituted much of its cooking, claiming it for their own.

I have never had a chocolate cake I have liked as much as my mother's, however, one day, way down-island, I had this grand, delicately spiced cake.

12 tablespoons unsalted butter, softened to room temperature
1 1/2 cups granulated sugar
2 large eggs, room temperature
4 squares baking chocolate, melted over double boiler
1 1/2 cups all-purpose flour
1/4 teaspoon baking powder
1/4 teaspoon baking soda
1/4 cup cocoa powder
1 teaspoon instant coffee
1/8 teaspoon nutmeg
1/2 teaspoon cinnamon
1/4 cup whole milk
1/2 cup plus 2 tablespoons buttermilk
1/2 cup Orange Curacao liqueur (while on a cruise I visited the factory in Curacao where they manufacture this liqueur)
2 teaspoons good quality vanilla extract

Frosting:
4 ounces whipped cream cheese
1/2 cup butter
4 squares baking chocolate melted
1 cup powdered sugar, sifted
1 tablespoon unsweetened cocoa, powdered
3 tablespoons Curacao liqueur
1/2 teaspoon orange extract
1/2 teaspoon vanilla
1/8 teaspoon cinnamon

1 small tin Mandarin orange slices, carefully drained

Place oven rack in centerposition, removing all other racks. Heat oven to 350º. Grease two 8 x 1.5 inch round pans with vegetable shortening, dusting with cocoa powderinstead of flour. Cover bottom of pans with rounds of parchment paper,greasing and dusting this also. Shake out any excess cocoa powder.

In a large bowl using anelectric mixer (handheld OK) set at medium speed, beat butter untilfluffy, about 45 seconds. Slowly add sugar, beating an additional 4minutes. Add eggs one at a time, beating each 45 seconds. Very slowlydribble in slightly cooled melted chocolate, beat for 30 seconds.

In another bowl, sift flour,baking soda, baking powder, instant coffee, nutmeg and cinnamon.

In an oversize measuring cup orlarge coffee cup, combine, milk, buttermilk, liqueur and vanilla.

Put mixer at slowest speed andadd about π of the dry ingredients to the butter mixer. Then pour in about1/3 of the milk/liqueur mixture. Repeat until all ingredients areincorporated, scraping sides of bowl often. Stop mixing here. Remember tobeat slowly, you don't want to pump too much air into mixture, thecake will fall apart.

Pour batter into both pans.Bake until center is firm and a toothpick comes out clean (there will be afew crumbs), about 25 to 32 minutes.

Cool cakes, still in pan, onwire racks for 12 minutes. Gently slip a knife around cake edges,loosening sides. Remove parchment. Return to wire racks. When completelycool, frost as instructed under Chocolate Orange Curacao Cake.

Frosting:
With a hand beater set on low speed cream together the cream cheese, butter and melted chocolate. Increase speed gradually beating in the sifted sugar and cocoa powder. Add liqueur, vanilla, orange extract and cinnamon, beating until smooth and fluffy.

Frost the top of one layer cake and put the other on top of it. Frost the top and sides. Allow 35 to 40 minutes for the butter in the frosting to slightly harden in cool place, refrigerate if needed. Decoratively garnish with the Mandarin orange slices.

Yield: 1 cake, 8 to 12 servings

Banana Orange Nut Crème Caramel

Grand Cayman

Whenever traveling to visit my mother on the mainland, she is always amazed at the many uses of evaporated milk that I come up with. Low-fat evaporated milk has the added bonus of being full of calcium. One loses some of the creaminess with the low-fat version, so I like to mix it half with regular evaporated milk.

3 tablespoons water
1/3 cup granulated sugar
1/2 teaspoon fresh orange zest
1 tablespoon frozen orange juice concentrate
6 ounces evaporated milk
6 ounces fat-free evaporated milk
2 large eggs, beaten
1 large ripe banana, well mashed
2 tablespoons light or golden rum
1/4 teaspoon cinnamon
1/4 teaspoon cardamom
1/4 teaspoon salt
1/4 cup walnuts, toasted and finely crushed

Preheat oven to 325∞.

Coat 4 custard cups with cooking spray and set aside.

Combine sugar, zest, and water in a small heavy skillet over medium heat. Cook until sugar has caramelized (after about 3 to 4 minutes), stirring often. Pour the caramelized sugar into each of the four cups coating the bottom.

Combine remaining ingredients except the walnuts whisking until light. Pour into the custard cups. Place the custard cups in a large glass baking dish filled with water. Water should cover the bottom 1 inch of the cups.

Bake for approximately 45 minutes. A fork inserted in the center will come out clean. Remove cups, cool and refrigerate overnight to allow flavors to mingle.

Run a wet knife around the edge of the cups and invert onto pretty plates. Sprinkle with toasted nuts.

Yield: 4 servings

Did you know?: A company called Fry and Sons in 1847 created the first chocolate bar in England. Chocolate originated with the Mayans and later became an important part of ritual with the Aztecs as well. The word cacao comes from the Mayan word cacahuaquchtl, which was the tree of their gods. Cacao arrived in Africa in the early 1800's and still produces the majority of cacao in the world. The Swiss consume the most chocolate in the world, then Belgians, English and Germans. The cacao tree attains a height of 26 feet and produces continually during the year. Beans are produced in a pod, which must be processed. First fermentation where the beans are subjected to heat up to 120∞F which activates the enzymes and kills harmful pathogens. The beans are then dried to further reduce moisture. Then carefully picking over will reduces twigs and stones. Roasting will now remove some of the tannins and make for a milder flavor. Cracking with steel rollers will remove the bean from the shell, leaving a sticky paste called chocolate mass. The mass is further pressed to remove the fat, or cocoa butter. The remaining paste is further rolled, leaving cocoa powder. Of interest is that white chocolate does not contain cocoa liqueur. It uses the cocoa butter and adds evaporated milk, sugar, and vanilla. Cocoa contains fat, carbohydrates, protein, caffeine, as well as minute amounts of minerals.

Purchasing: Look for high-quality chocolate free of white spots or bubbles. It should have a delectable aroma and be brown in color, not grayish.

Storing: Keep in a cool place for several months. If refrigerated expect a white cast to the chocolate, which is actually the cocoa butter rising. It will taste relatively the same, just look a bit odd.

Preparation: Keep moisture away from the chocolate when cooking otherwise it will cause a reaction and clump. Cooking will intensify the flavor, but do not go over 120∞F. Use a double boiler for best results and heat slowly.

Rum Lime Chocolate Soufflé with Caramel Sauce
St. John, U.S. Virgin Islands

Some of the best restaurants in the U.S. Virgin Islands are located on sleepy St. John. Most of this luxuriant island has been designated a National Park.

1 tablespoon butter
1 tablespoon granulated sugar
1/2 cup unsweetened cocoa powder
6 tablespoons hot water
2 tablespoons butter
3 tablespoons all-purpose flour
1 teaspoon lime zest
1 tablespoons fresh lime juice
1 tablespoon dark rum
2/3 cup milk
1/4 cup granulated sugar
1/8 teaspoon salt
4 large egg whites
3 tablespoons sugar

sauce:
1/2 cup granulated sugar
5 tablespoons hot water
1 tablespoon butter

Chill a medium glass bowl for the egg whites.

Preheat oven to 375∞.

Using the 1 tablespoon of butter, evenly coat a 1 1/2 quart soufflé dish, sprinkle the 1 tablespoon sugar, and shake to coat bottom and sides evenly. Put aside.

Combine the cocoa powder and hot water in a large bowl and set aside.

Select a medium heavy saucepan, melt the 2 tablespoons butter, add flour, and cook for 1 minute stirring steadily. Add lime zest, juice, rum, milk, 1/2 cup sugar, and salt, cooking several minutes over medium heat until thick. Remove pot from heat and stir in cocoa mix. Pour this into the large bowl that originally held the cocoa.

Beat egg whites for 1 minute and gradually add in the 3 tablespoons sugar. Beat until stiff. Fold in the egg white 1/3 at a time into the cocoa mixture carefully. Pour into soufflé dish.

Bake for 35 minutes until top is slightly crunchy. Serve at once with Caramel Sauce.

Caramel Sauce:

In a small heavy sauce pan stir the sugar into the hot water, stirring constantly over medium heat until sugar has browned slightly and caramelized. Stir in the butter until melted and remove from heat. Allow to cool for 2 minutes and spoon over the soufflé.

Yield: 6 servings

Black Bottom Orange-Mango Tart
Martinique

This pleasing tart was found in a fabulous restaurant in Martinique. I recall having to jog quite a bit when I returned from that trip—all my willpower disappeared mysteriously. Much of the work is taken out of this recipe by using the store-bought chocolate graham crackers.

Crust:
1 1/4 cup crushed chocolate graham crackers
1/4 cup finely crushed walnuts (should be powdery)
1/4 cup granulated sugar
1/3 cup melted butter

filling:

1 package orange Jell-O mix
1/2 cup boiling water
1/2 cup orange juice
3 ounces cream cheese
1/4 cup sugar
2 cups fresh mango sent through a food processor until smooth
1 pint heavy cream, whipped until firm peaks form

To make crust, assemble all ingredients and mix in medium bowl. Press into a lightly buttered glass pie dish. Bake at 350 degrees for 10 minutes; remove and set aside.

To make filling: Dissolve the Jell-O in 1/2 cup boiling water, adding in the orange juice as well. With an electric hand beater, combine the cream cheese, sugar, and mango until smooth. Gradually mix in the Jell-O and fold in the whipped cream. Pour into the graham crust and chill until firm, approximately four hours.

Yield: 6 to 8 servings

Island Speak: I talkin' lapias, mon. Translation: I'm talking a long time ago, in the old days, man.

White Chocolate Cake with Coconut Frosting
St. Martin

Remember these wonderful candy bars as a child? These were the ones with the sweet coconut insides, chocolate shell, and two huge almonds on top. This desert is made with white chocolate and garnished on the outside with coconut, contributing to its elegant appearance.

2 cups cake flour, sifted
2 1/2 teaspoons baking powder
1/4 teaspoon salt
3/4 cup evaporated milk
4 ounces white baking chocolate
1 1/2 teaspoons vanilla
5 egg yolks
1/2 cup butter
1 tablespoon lemon zest, fresh
1/2 teaspoon lemon extract
1 cup granulated sugar
1/8 teaspoon cardamom
5 egg whites
1/2 teaspoon cream of tartar

Frosting:

3 egg whites
1/2 teaspoon cream of tartar
1 1/2 cups sugar
4 ounces white baking chocolate, melted
1 teaspoon vanilla
1 small package grated sweetened coconut

Preheat oven to 350 degrees. Grease and flour two standard 9 inch cake pans.

Sift together the flour, baking powder, and salt.

In a double boiler or in a small saucepan over gentle heat, melt together the evaporated milk, chocolate and vanilla. Be careful to just melt and combine the chocolate with the milk to avoid scorching which will give it an undesirable flavor.

Cream together the egg yolks, butter, lemon zest and extract, plus 1 cup granulated sugar. Gradually stir in the chocolate mixture and cardamom. With an electric beater set on low speed slowly add the flour mixture until smooth. Do not over beat.

Beat the egg whites with a pinch of cream of tartar until glossy stiff peaks form. Fold this into the batter carefully. Pour batter into pans, baking for 30 minutes or so until a toothpick emerges clean out of the cakes.

Cook cakes in their pans for 15 minutes. Invert on wire racks until completely cooled.

To make frosting; in a medium bowl beat the 3 egg whites with the cream of tartar until stiff. Fold in the sugar. Beat constantly, adding in the melted chocolate and vanilla. Blend vigorously and remove from heat, allowing to cool for 15 minutes.

Frost top of one cake layer and sprinkle thickly with the grated coconut. Place second cake on top of the first and frost sides first then the top. Again, sprinkle liberally with grated coconut.

Yield: 12 servings

TIP: Add the sugar to the lightly beaten egg whites one or two teaspoons at a time. Beat on high speed until stiff, glossy peaks are formed. To test that all the sugar has dissolved, rub a bit of the egg mixture between your thumb and forefinger; it should be even and not gritty.

Mango Passionfruit Upside-Down Cake
Aruba

Most of us have had, yawn, ho-hum, Pineapple Upside-Down Cake. Well, I can't say this version won't make you a little bit sleepy as the recipe calls for plenty of spirits, and not the kind that knock on walls either. The exotic fruits in this cake will produce a veritable Caribbean carnival in your mouth.

filling:
3 tablespoons butter
1/3 cup firmly packed brown sugar
1/2 teaspoon rum extract
1/2 cup any good Caribbean rum
3 tablespoons passion fruit concentrate (from frozen food section)
1 cup fresh mango, chopped

1 1/2 cups cake flour, sifted
1/4 teaspoon salt
2 teaspoons baking powder
2 eggs
3/4 cup granulated sugar
1/2 cup butter
1/2 teaspoon vanilla extract
3/4 cup buttermilk

In a small sauce pan melt the butter for the filling and stir in brown sugar, rum extract, rum, passion fruit concentrate and chopped mangos. Simmer for 1 minute and pour into either a glass pie dish or standard 9-inch baking pan.

In a large bowl, sift together flour, salt, and baking powder. In a separate bowl, cream the eggs, butter, sugar and vanilla and almond extracts. With an electric beater, whisk in the buttermilk. Gradually beat the flour into the egg mixture until smooth; do not over beat.

Pour this over the mango mixture and bake at 350 degrees for 30 minutes until an inserted toothpick comes out clean.

Cool in pan for ten minutes. Using a fork poke holes randomly through the top of cake. Pour the rum over cake and through the holes, allowing sitting for 10 minutes. Put a plate over the top of the cake, shake gently, and invert cake. Scrape any remaining fruit topping onto cake.

Serve warm with vanilla ice cream or whipped cream.

Yield: 6 servings

Did you know?: Kumquats make an excellent substitute for lemons or limes? You can eat the entire fruit as there is no need to peel it. The skin is actually more palatable then the tart meat. This tree originated in China and will grow up to 20 feet high. Fruits are very tiny, 1 or 2 inches in length and resemble miniature oranges.
Purchasing: Choose unblemished fruits that are firm as they are quite fragile.
Storing: Best if kept refrigerated; will last about 3 weeks then.

Kumquat Meringue Nests

Barbados

Meringue:
4 egg whites at room temperature
1/4 teaspoon cream of tartar
few grains of salt
1/2 teaspoon vanilla extract
1/4 teaspoon orange extract
1/2 cup sugar

Filling:
3 eggs
1 egg yolk
1 tin sweetened and condensed milk
1/2 cup sugar
2/3 cups minced and pureed fresh kumquats
2 tablespoons fresh lemon juice
2 tablespoons fresh lime juice
1 tablespoon orange juice concentrate
small package of sweetened grated coconut

TIP: Do not attempt to make any sort of stiff meringue on a rainy or humid day. They simply will not hold their shape and become tough and soggy.

Preheat oven to 300 degrees. Line a baking sheet with either plain brown paper or wax paper. Using the top of a peanut butter lid, trace circles a couple of inches apart on the paper.

Beat the room temperature egg whites, cream of tartar, salt, vanilla and orange extract using a portable hand mixer set on low. When soft peaks begin to form, add the sugar one tablespoon at a time, increasing speed to high until stiff peaks have formed and the meringue looks glossy. Put the meringue into a pastry bag. Start at the center of each circle and trace ever larger circles until you reach the edge. Once the edge has been met, keep going round until the sides are built up approximately an 1 1/2 inches, just like a bird's nest. Bake in oven for 45 minutes until dry. Allow shells to remain in oven for an hour.

Filling: In a medium bowl beat the eggs, milk, and sugar until frothy. Add the kumquat and juices. Over gentle heat in a medium saucepan, heat until mixture thickens. Allow to cool and refrigerate for 2 hours.

Sprinkle the coconut lightly into the bottom of the meringue, allowing some to spill up and over the sides. Spoon the chilled filling into the meringues. Finish garnishing with a little coconut around the edges to resemble the twigs in the nest.

Yield: 6 to 7 meringues

Puerto Rican Orange Flan
Puerto Rico

This is possibly the most popular Hispanic dessert and variations of it can be found in all the Spanish-speaking islands such as Cuba, Puerto Rico, and Santa Domingo.

Caramel:
1 1/4 cup granulated sugar
1/3 cup water and more as needed
1 teaspoon orange extract

Flan:
8 large eggs
2 egg yolks
1 cup sugar
1 1/2 tablespoons fresh zest of orange
1 teaspoon vanilla extract
4 cups milk

one tin mandarin orange sections for garnish

Preheat oven to 300 degrees.

You need to work quickly with the caramel once it has turned a golden color. If it becomes too stiff to work with, add a little hot water. In a medium saucepan, heat the water and sugar to a boil. Reduce heat and continue cooking until color deepens, adding orange extract. Pour into 10 custard cups, tilting so all sides and bottom are coated.

Flan: In a small bowl beat the eggs, sugar, orange zest, and vanilla. In a medium saucepan, scald the milk and remove from heat. Beat the milk gradually into the egg mixture, stirring in orange extract. Spoon the flan into the custard cups.

Place the cups into a baking dish, with hot water coming 2/3 up the sides of the cups. Bake 45 minutes to an hour—a fork should come out clean from the center. Allow to cool on rack until room temperature. Wrap securely with wax or plastic wrap and refrigerate until chilled.

Run a knife dipped in warm water around the edge of the cups to loosen.

Shake gently and invert onto desert plates, pouring caramel over the top of each flan. Garnish with mandarin orange sections.

Yield: 10 flan

Island Speak: Shavin blows
Translation: To cuff or hit someone

West Indian Christmas Pudding

St. Thomas, U.S. Virgin Islands

This delicious pudding appears to be another one of those 'borrowed and exchanged' European recipes and reminds me of English bread pudding.

4 cups fresh white breadcrumbs (I like to leave them a bit lumpy)
1/3 cup of almonds, powdered
1/3 cup cashews, powdered
1/2 cup sugar
6 eggs, beaten
1 teaspoon vanilla
1 teaspoon almond extract
1/2 teaspoon cinnamon
2 tablespoons fresh orange zest
1 tablespoon fresh lime zest
1 tablespoon fresh lemon zest
2 cups milk
1/2 cup raisins
1 cup rum
whipped cream

Toast the breadcrumbs in the oven until just dry. Line a 9-inch square or round baking dish with the breadcrumbs. I prefer the square as it is easier to cut serving portions.

In a small bowl, combine the nuts and sugar. Set aside.

In a large bowl using a portable mixer, combine the eggs, extracts, spices, zest, and milk. Fold in raisins. Pour over the breadcrumbs. Sprinkle the nut mixture over this.

Bake for 45 minutes. Remove from oven and allow cooling for 10 minutes. Score random holes with a fork and pour rum over top of pudding. Serve warm with whipped cream.

Yield: 8 servings

Rum Mango Blueberry Brulee
Barbados

Mount Gay rum comes from this former sugarcane plantation island. Use this rum for authentic flavor.

1/3 cup light rum
1/2 teaspoon vanilla
1/3 cup orange juice concentrate
1/2 teaspoon cinnamon
5 tablespoons granulated sugar
butter to grease 8 inch glass dish
1 1/2 pound cubed mango, drained
2 large ripe pears, peeled, cored, and diced
1 pint blueberries
8 egg yolks, chilled
8 tablespoons granulated sugar
1 1/2 cups whipping cream chilled
1 teaspoon orange zest
6 tablespoons brown sugar
whipped cream

In a small bowl combine rum, vanilla, orange juice concentrate, cinnamon and 5 tablespoons of sugar.

Butter an 8 inch glass dish, square, or round and arrange cubed mango, pear, and blueberries. Pour rum mixture over fruit.

In a bowl, hand beat the yolks until frothy, adding sugar gradually. Whisk in cream and orange zest. Pour this over the fruit. Sprinkle brown sugar over top.

Set glass dish inside of a larger dish, filled with water. Bake at 275° until set, about 45 to 50 minutes.

Serve with generous dollops of whipped cream.

Yield: 6 servings

Did you know?: Mangoes were long unknown outside Asia? In cultivation for over 6000 years, they are thought to have originated in India. In the 18th century, Portuguese explorers brought the mango to Brazil and hence the fruit spread to the rest of the world. The fruit grows on trees in tropical climates attaining up to 100 feet in height and are related to the cashew and pistachio. They are 82% water, excellent source of vitamin A and C, good source of potassium and copper. Do not eat the skin as it can be irritating to the mucous membranes.

Purchasing: Choose fruit that will yield slightly to a gentle pressure, black spots indicate extreme ripeness. Do not choose fruit that is rock hard.

Storing: Leave unripe fruit to reach its peak at room temperature. With my experience, ripe fruits will last no longer than a week in the refrigerator.

Preparation: Make four cuts from top to bottom on the fruit. Peel back and pull down skin. Using a long sharp knife, slice off the meat and cube, being careful of the large woody pit.

Lime Rum Gingersnap Cookies
British Virgin Islands

Make these delicious sweet and crunchy cookies as a light after dinner finale or use in the following recipe for Frozen Tropical Fruit Pie with Pineapple Salsa

1 cup unsalted butter, softened
1 1/2 cups granulated sugar
1 egg
1 tablespoon light or dark rum
2 tablespoons Rose's limejuice
1 teaspoon freshly grated lime zest
1 1/2 tablespoons freshly grated ginger
3 1/4 cups plus 2 tablespoons all-purpose flour
2 teaspoons baking soda
1 teaspoon ground ginger
1/2 teaspoon ground cinnamon
1/2 teaspoon ground cloves

In a large bowl beat, the butter with the sugar, adding the egg, beat until fluffy. Stir in rum, lime juice, zest, and ginger. Sift together dry ingredients and add to bowl until well combined.

Cut dough in half and form into a roll. Wrap with wax paper and chill overnight until firm.

Preheat oven to 350 degrees. Lightly grease baking sheets or use non-stick ones.
Slice rolls thinly slightly less than 1/4 inch. Place on cookie sheets leaving at least 1 1/2 inches space between cookies. Sprinkle sugar over the tops of cookies and bake until golden about 12 to 15 minutes. Remove cookies from oven and allow to cool on sheet for 8 to 10 minutes. Cookies will have hardened slightly and be easier to remove with a metal spatula. Allow cooking on a wire rack.

Yield: 75 to 80 cookies

Island Speak: "Limin'" means hanging out, playing, just cooling out.

Frozen Tropical Pie with Pineapple Salsa
Anguilla

This pie is so good after a hot, spicy tropical meal—a sure crowd pleaser in the heat of the summer! The rum adds a little extra kick.

3 cups frozen mango chunks
1/4 cup light rum
3/4 light cream
2 tablespoons corn syrup
1 teaspoon vanilla
1/4 cup granulated sugar
4 tablespoons butter, melted
1 1/2 cups crushed Lime Rum Gingersnap cookies
1/4 teaspoon ground cinnamon
12 to 15 extra cookies

for the salsa:
1 cup finely diced pineapple chunks
2 kiwis, peeled and chopped
juice of one lemon
2 tablespoons rum
1 tablespoon corn syrup
1 cup fresh raspberries

In a food processor, combine the mango, rum, cream, corn syrup, vanilla, and sugar. Freeze for 2 hours.

In a small bowl, mix the melted butter and crushed cookies with the cinnamon. Press this into the bottom of a 9 inch pie plate, preferably glass. Place in the freezer while preparing remaining ingredients.

To make salsa, in a large bowl gently toss the pineapple and kiwi. In a small cup, stir the lemon juice, rum, and corn syrup. Pour over fruit. Gently fold in the raspberries. Set aside.

Remove the mango mixture from the freezer and spoon into the food processor. Whip thoroughly. Spoon this onto the cookie crust and garnish with cookies.

Cut into wedges and serve with salsa.

Yield: 8 servings

Island Speak: Melee means creating gossip or confusion.

Cointreau Lemon Tart

Guadeloupe

This French island has a population of approximately 410,000, its official language is French, and the capital is Basse-Terre.

for crust:
1 cup crushed graham crackers
1/2 cup unsalted butter, melted
1/4 cup finely crushed almonds
2 tablespoons granulated sugar
3 tablespoons marzipan

for filling:
8 lemons
4 egg yolks
1 14-ounce can sweetened condensed milk
1/4 cup Cointreau
1 teaspoons fresh lemon zest
3 egg whites
1 tablespoon sugar
crème fraiche

Preheat oven to 325 degrees and chill a small glass bowl in refrigerator.

In a small bowl, combine the crushed crackers, butter, almonds, marzipan, and sugar. Using a pastry cutter or fork, cut in the marzipan. Press onto the bottom and sides of a 9-inch pie pan.

Juice the lemons and pour into a large bowl. Using an electric mixer, blend in on high speed the egg yolks, condensed milk, Cointreau and lemon zest.

Wash off the mixer blades, using the chilled bowl beat the egg whites and sugar until stiff peaks have formed. Fold into the condensed milk mixture.

Spoon into the pie crust and bake for about 30 minutes. Cool completely and refrigerate for several hours. Serve with generous dollops of crème fraiche and strong hot coffee.

Yield: Serves 6

Drinks

Bar-tending in the Islands

Think of Caribbean cocktails and the likes of Planter's Punch, Banana Daiquiris and Yellow Bird come to mind . This chapter explores the exotic flavor and essences of Caribbean spirits, primarily rums of the islands and the new flavored rums, which no one seems to know what to do with. Many of the drinks may be familiar to you, but just did not know the actual ingredients or correct proportions. In addition, when I wrote "Just Add Rum!" there were so many tempting drinks made without rum that had no place in that book. A concise and basic selection of these is presented as well. Read the basic instructions and stocking suggestions—above all remember bartending is another one of those skills that improves with time and practice. Enjoy!

Basic Bar Stock for a Caribbean Bar

Liquors:

White rum
Gold rum
Dark rum
151- proof rum
Coconut rum
Banana rum
Pineapple rum
Vodka
Gin
Scotch and rye whiskey
Bourbon
Brandy or cognac
Vermouth (both sweet and dry)
Tequila
Contreau
Irish Crème Liqueur
Galliano
Cherry Brandy
Crème de Cacao
Crème de Menthe (both green and white)
Drambuie
Curacao
Coffee liqueur
Grand Marnier
Sambucca
B & B
Frangelico
Amaretto
Peach schnapps
Crème de Cassis
Triple Sec

Soft drinks:

ginger ale
coca cola (diet is nice as well)
soda water
lemon or lime soda
tonic water
orange juice
grapefruit juice
pineapple juice
lemon and limejuice
tomato juice
cranberry juice
milk
cream

Fruits and garnishes:

oranges
lemons
limes
pineapple slices
maraschino cherries
olives
cocktail onions
mint
cinnamon
nutmeg
sugar (powdered and granulated)
simple syrup
salt
cayenne
horseradish

Utensils:

clean ice
cocktail napkins
stirrers
cocktail shaker and strainer
electric blender

corkscrew
grater for nutmeg
spoons
sharp paring knife for lemon and lime twists
straws
ice bucket and tongs

Miscellaneous

angostura bitters
Tabasco
Worcestershire
Grenadine
Rose's limejuice
Cream of coconut

Tips and Suggestions

All cloudy drinks, including cream drinks should be shaken. Never shake a drink with carbonated water or soda. Most clear drinks are stirred, unless specified otherwise. On some drinks, such as a martini, your guest will let you know shaken or stirred.

Use only fresh clean ice and fruit juice

Chill glasses before serving, either in the freezer or by swishing full of ice—then pouring the ice out.

Serve all cold drinks ice cold, and hot drinks, hot.

Carbonated water or soda should be the last ingredient added to a drink.

Measure carefully, never 'free pour'. You could end up with a few overnight guests!

Use sparkling clean and unchipped glassware.
Place garnish on drink, i.e. cherry, lemon zest, etc. last, just before serving.

Use tongs for ice, not your hands.

Angel's Hell

British Virgin Islands

Pusser's rum is to the British Virgin Islands as Cruzan to St. Croix and Bacardi to Puerto Rico.

1oz. Pusser's Rum
1 oz. Crème de Cassis
1 oz. Blue Curacao
1 oz. light cream

Layer this drink into a glass as follows: Crème de Cassis (hell), rum (purgatory), Blue Curacao (gates of heaven) and cream (heaven). Voila!

Bahama Mama

Nassua

While visiting Nassau, this famous drink was found on nearly every bar and restaurant menu!

1 oz. light or dark rum
1 oz. cherry brandy
2 oz. pineapple juice
2 oz. orange juice
juice of 1/2 lemon
1 teaspoon powdered sugar
crushed ice

Shake all ingredients except the ice well. Serve in a frosted glass over crushed ice. Garnish with a pineapple wedge.

Banana Daiquiri

St. Thomas, U.S. Virgin Islands

The island of St. Thomas is famous for it's banana daiquiris. This is one of the easier and more basic recipes that works.

1 large ripe banana
2 oz. dark rum or gold
splash of Triple Sec
juice of one lime
1 oz. light cream
1/2 oz. simple syrup
crushed ice

In a blender, pour in the liquid ingredients first, and then add the banana, broken up. Once pureed smooth, add small amounts of ice until the desired consistency is reached. Pour into tall tulip-shaped glass.

Banaquit

Martinique

Banaquits are lovely bright yellow finch-like birds found in the Caribbean. They just love sugar.

1 oz. Galliano
1 oz. light rum
1 oz. orange juice
1 oz. light cream
crushed ice

In a shaker, combine all ingredients well. Serve either straight up or over crushed ice.

Beached Sailor

Cayman Islands

Columbus named these islands Las Tortugas when he noticed all the turtles swimming around the islands. The Caymans with their caves and coves are replete with tales of piracy. Only 480 miles south of Miami and close to Jamaica, it is one of the most popular destinations in the Eastern Caribbean.

1 oz. light rum
1/2 oz. apricot brandy
1/2 teaspoon Rose's limejuice
2 oz. light cream

Put all ingredients in a shaker and mix. Pour over ice in a rocks glass.

Bermuda Sunset

Bermuda

1 oz. grenadine
1 oz. orange juice
1 oz. gold rum
1 oz. champagne

See if you can find a margarita glass for this one, as the layers are especially attractive.

Pour the ingredients in the order listed, being careful not to disturb each layer.

Blackbeard's Tropical Spiced Tea

St. Thomas, U.S. Virgin Islands

1 1/2 oz. Captain Morgan's Spiced Rum
1 oz. Coca cola
1 oz. Lemon soda
4 oz. Iced tea

Pour each ingredient into a tall glass over ice. Stir gently. Garnish with a mint leaf or lemon wedge.

Blue Lagoon

St. Barthelemy

The enchantment of St. Barth's is the result of the unique combination of the tropical Caribbean and French culture.

1/2 oz. Blue Curacao
1 1/2 oz. vodka
1 oz. freshly squeezed lemon juice
1 oz. simple syrup

Shake all ingredients with ice. Strain into a rocks glass.

Brown-eyed girl

Puerto Rico

1 oz. dark rum
1 oz. Kahlua
1 oz. Bailey's Irish Cream
1 oz. light cream

Puerto Rico is a huge (110 by 35) diversified island. From El Yunque, its 28,000-acre rainforest, hundreds of beaches and Spanish architecture, there is something for everyone. I really love Old San Juan with its cobblestone streets, charming hideaway restaurants, and stonewalls.

Using a shaker with a strainer fitted over the top, fill with ice, dark rum, and Kahlua. Shake and strain into a rocks glass. Carefully pour first the Bailey's, then the cream.

Buccaneer's brew

St. Kitts

This drink has always reminded me of the cherry cokes I loved as a kid. The island of St. Kitts is about 65 square miles, but not short on verdant beauty. It is lush, mountainous, complete with rainforests and dazzling water-falls.

1 1/2 oz. dark rum
1 tablespoon Grenadine
6 oz. cola
lime wedge

Gently stir all ingredients and pour into a tall glass over ice. Squeeze the lime slice into the drink and toss in.

Bushwacker

Antigua

Grinding your own fresh nutmeg really is the best for these recipes. Makes a good liquid lunch.

1 oz. dark rum
1 oz. coconut rum
1 oz. chocolate liqueur
1/2 oz. coffee liqueur
1 oz. Bailey's Irish Cream liqueur
crushed ice
nutmeg

Fill a blender with slightly less than 1 cup crushed ice. Add all ingredients except the nutmeg and blend until an ice cream consistency is attained. Sprinkle with ground nutmeg.

Caribbean Grass Hopper

St. Thomas, U.S. Virgin Islands

1 oz. White Crème de Cacao
1 oz. Green Crème de Menthe
1 oz. Coco Lopez or cream of coconut
1 oz. Fresh milk

Shake all ingredients vigorously and serve over ice or straight up.

Caribbean Lover

Curacao

1 oz. white rum
1 oz. dark Crème de Cacao

Shake in a strainer with ice and pour into a shot glass.

Deep Blue Sea

St. John, U. S. Virgin Islands

One of the first things one notices about the Caribbean is the incredible clarity of the water and the deep aquamarine jewel-like color.

3/4 oz. Blue Curacao
1 oz. pineapple rum
1/2 oz. Triple Sec
4 oz. sweet and sour mix

Shake all ingredients well and pour over ice into a tall glass.

El Coqui
Puerto Rico

The coqui is a tiny tree frog that inhabits only Puerto Rico and has become outrageously popular. Once I had an apartment in San Juan, and the chirping 'kokee, kokee' from these amphibians was so loud that I could barely hear on the telephone. Also, he is not bright lime green as depicted by the souvenir shops, but more like a golden tan, hence the orange juice in this drink tempers the green of the Midori.

1 oz. Midori
1 oz. white rum
juice of one lime
fresh zest of lime
4 oz. orange juice

Pour all ingredients except the zest, into a tall glass filled 1/2 full with ice. Using a long stirrer, blend all ingredients well until a pale mud-like color is achieved. Sprinkle sparingly with lime zest.

Great White
Turks and Caicos

I read somewhere that your chances of being attacked by a shark were 1 in 20 million. Actually being struck be lightning was a lot higher on the scale.

1 oz. white rum
1 oz. Cointreau
2 oz. lemon soda

Fill a rocks glass with ice and gently stir in the above ingredients. Garnish with an orange slice.

Guadeloupe Sling
Guadeloupe

1 1/2 oz. gin
1/2 oz. mango rum
1/2 oz. cherry brandy
juice of 1/2 a lemon
dash of angostura bitters
club soda

This is another one of those innocuously smooth-tasting drinks, where before you know it, you've got several under your belt.

Shake all ingredients except the club soda and pour over ice into a tall glass. Top with club soda and garnish with an orange slice and maraschino cherry.

Hot Chili Pepper
Trinidad & Tobago

The Caribbean islands have made the map with their abundant use of fiery chili peppers. Enjoy the sweet, sour and spicy here!

1 oz. Mango Rum
1/2 oz. Peach Schnapps
splash of jalapeno juice

Shake all ingredients with ice and strain into a shot glass.

Mai-Tai

Aruba

Refreshing, yet traditional version of the fabled original.

2 oz. light rum
1 oz. Curacao
1/2 oz. Amaretto
juice of 1/2 a lime
1 oz. simple syrup
1 tablespoon Grenadine

Shake with ice and strain into an old-fashioned glass, either straight up or partially filled with ice.

Morgan's Madness

Antigua

Dangerous and no more to be said!

2 oz. Captain Morgan's Spiced Rum
1/2 oz. Amaretto
1/2 oz. white Crème de Cacao
splash of Grand Marnier

Shake rum, Amaretto and Crème de Cacao with ice and strain into a rocks glass. Float the Grand Marnier on top.

Mudslide

Bermuda

1/2 oz. Coffee Liqueur
1/2 oz. Irish Cream Liqueur
1 oz. vodka
drop of Grand Marnier
cola

Fill a tall glass half full with ice. Pour in the liqueurs and vodka, stir gently. Fill to top with cola and float a little Grand Marnier.

Painkiller

British Virgin Islands

2 oz. 151 proof rum
2 oz. pineapple juice
2 oz. orange juice
splash of Coco Lopez or cream of coconut
crushed ice
nutmeg

I had to swim to the bar to get this drink, as there is no boat dock at White Bay, Jost Van Dyke. It is quite easy to drink too many of these while swinging in a hammock.

Shake all ingredients except the nutmeg well and pour over crushed ice. Garnish with freshly grated nutmeg.

Peach Colada

Aruba

1/2 cup diced fresh, frozen, or canned peaches
1 1/2 oz. crème of coconut
2 oz. light or gold rum
splash of Rose's lime juice
crushed ice

Place all ingredients in blender until smooth. Pour into a large tulip-shaped glass. Garnish with a mint leaf.

Pina Colada

Barbados

No one quite knows where the first Pina Colada originated. This is a basic recipe.

2 oz. light or gold rum
2 oz. pineapple juice
1 1/2 oz. crème of coconut
crushed ice

Place all ingredients in blender along with one cup of crushed ice. Blend well and serve in a tall fancy glass.

Pink Oleander

St. Martin, French West Indies

Oleander is a lovely pink flower that grows profusely on shrubs that can reach 12 feet in height. They also grow in white and yellow.

1 oz. white Crème de Cacao
1 oz. Blackberry Brandy
dash of Triple Sec
1 oz. milk

Shake all ingredients well and pour over ice into a rocks glass.

Planter's punch

Jamaica

1 1/2 oz. gold or dark rum
2 oz. simple syrup
juice of one lime
one maraschino cherry
and big splash of the cherry juice

Enjoy sipping the national drink of the islands during lazy summer weekends. Orange juice may be substituted for the simple syrup.

Pour all ingredients over ice in a tall glass and stir. Garnish with cherry.

Puerto Rican Parrot

Puerto Rico

1 oz. Midori
1 oz. Galliano
1/2 oz. Grenadine
1 oz. white rum

There are only about 40 Puerto Rican parrots left in El Yunque, Puerto Rico's tropical rainforest. These beautiful amazons are on the endangered species list and much loved on the island. Place the glass in front of your guest or customers, pouring the drink on the spot so as not to mix the colors unduly.

Use a spoon to layer the ingredients into a short tumbler. Fill halfway full of ice and first pour in the Grenadine. Using the spoon, pour the Midori over the bowl of the spoon slowly to not disturb the Grenadine underneath. Do the same for the Galliano and float the white rum on the top.

Rum Punch

Guadeloupe

This drink is truly refreshing. As the alcohol is cleverly disguised, exercise caution.

1 oz. pineapple juice
1 oz. orange juice
1 oz. freshly squeezed lemon or limejuice
1/2 oz Grenadine
2 oz. light or gold rum

Shake all ingredients well. Pour over tall glass filled with ice.

Sex on the beach

Grenada

1/2 oz. Chambord
1/2 oz. Midori
1 oz. pineapple vodka

Yes, this does have an interesting name, doesn't it?

Shake all ingredients well and serve either straight up or on the rocks.

Silk panties

Jamaica

1 oz. vodka
1 oz. Mango rum or Peach Schnapps

Pour into a shaker filled with ice. Strain into a rocks glass.

Slippery nipple

Grand Cayman

1 oz. Sambuca
1 oz. Bailey's Irish Cream Liqueur
ground nutmeg
orange zest

Pour into a rock glass, stir. Dust with ground nutmeg and orange zest.

Steel pan

St. Croix, U.S. Virgin Islands

1 oz. passion fruit vodka
1 oz. white rum
4 oz. passion fruit juice
granulated sugar

Warning! Warning! These drinks are so smooth, you'll think you are drinking a fruit drink instead of one heavily laced with alcohol and your head will feel like steel pans are beating in it the next day. Steel pan music is strongly promoted in the islands and actually taught as part of the music program in many schools.

Wet the lip of a rocks glass and twist in the granulated sugar. Fill the glass with ice and pour in all the ingredients, stirring gently.

Swingin' Iguana

Dominican Republic

Take care when layering this very pretty drink.

1 oz. green Chartreuse
1 oz. light rum
1/2 oz. Rose's limejuice
splash of orange juice
grated lime zest

In a rocks glass, using a spoon, carefully pour the Chartreuse over the spoon. Follow with the light rum, Rose's lime juice and carefully float a splash of the orange juice over the top. Mature iguanas have brown speckles on their backs. Sprinkle a bit of lime zest for taste and garnish over the top.

Tropical Cappuccino
Nassau Bahamas

1 1/2 oz. Kahlua
1 oz. Rum Cream liquor (similar to Irish Cream liquor, but with a rum base)
4 oz. cold coffee
splash of Chambord

Fill a tall glass 1/2 with ice. Pour in coffee, Rum Cream and Kahlua, stirring well. Gently float the Chambord on the top.

Yellow Bird
Nassau, Bahamas

1 oz. light rum
1/2 oz. pineapple rum
1/2 oz. crème de banana liquor
splash of Galliano
2 oz. pineapple juice
2 oz. orange juice

I love this tourist song that they named this drink after. Be sure to buy a CD of this and play while serving drinks to impart the correct atmosphere.

Shake all ingredients vigorously and pour into a tall glass filled with ice.

Zombie

Puerto Rico

Ok, if you've read Just Add Rum! you would know that I first had this drink when I was 18 years old in Nantucket, an island off the coast of Massachusetts. Here is the latest and best (1/2) version yet.

1 oz. Mango rum
1/2 oz. Pineapple rum
1/2 oz. Banana rum
1/2 oz. 151 proof rum
2 oz. orange juice
2 oz. pineapple juice
splash of Galliano and Chambord

Put all ingredients in the blender and fill with about 1 cup of crushed ice. Whirl until a slush-like consistency is achieved.

Caribbean Grocery Glossary

Don't be intimidated by some of the exotic ingredients in this cookbook. These very same ingredients make Caribbean cuisine colorful, aromatic and generally appealing both to the olfactory and visual senses. Ironically, during my last stateside trip I noticed that the groceries stores were often better stocked than our markets at home. Ingredients from all over the Caribbean and abroad had been readily imported and filled exotic displays to bursting. Wherever appropriate, I have included a substitution for an ingredient as well.

Accra: Very spicy fritter made from salt cod.

Ackee: This fruit grows on lovely trees. Be aware that the unripe fruit is poisonous. Very often served with salt fish (cod).

Achiote: Also known as annatto, these small brick red seeds have a spicy smoky flavor and are also used in the food industry to color cheese, margarine and other foods. Used extensively in Spanish cooking. *Paprika and saffron may be used as a substitute.*

Allspice: One of the main ingredients in jerk, this nutmeg-like spice is produced from small berries of the evergreen pimento tree, part of the myrtle family which is Native to the Caribbean and Amazon. Not to be confused with pimento used to stuff olives with, which is actually a capsicum pepper.

Avocado: Avocados originally came from South America and Mexico. Archeologists have found avocado seeds in burial grounds dating as early as 750 B.C.

Bammy: A type of pancake made from grated cassava root, often found in Jamaica.

Beans: Beans are one of the oldest and most nutritious foods known to mankind, being found in Peru almost 8000 years ago. High in protein, low in fat and cholesterol, they make a valuable basis for many Caribbean dishes.

Breadfruit: Large round fruit with leathery skin similar to a sweet potatoe often used as a substitute for potato.

Cashew: Another shrub native to the Caribbean and Brazil, it produces a red-yellow fruit from which the shell of the cashew nut grows out of. The shell of the nut is dangerously toxic, however the roasting process removes the poison.

Cassava: This root vegetable related to the poinsettia is also known as tapioca, manioc or yucca and must be cooked or baked before consumption as the juices contain a deadly cyanide-like poison. Cassava is made into fritters, bread and dumplings.

Channa: Garbanzo or chick peas.

Chayote: Member of the squash family small and light green in color, another name being christophene. One vine can produce literally more than one hundred chayotes. May be served raw in salads or cooked.

Cherimoya: Commonly known as the custard apple, the outside of the fruit resembles a leathery hand grenade. The pulp is a creamy white color the taste of strawberries with hard shiny black seeds.

Chicharron: Fried pork cracklings or skin.

Chili: Chili peppers originated in the Americas with evidence in Peru of their cultivation as far back as 2000 B.C. Chilies are high in vitamins A and C and were used by the Mayas, Incas and Aztec to add high flavor to cooking. From the mild bell pepper to the fiery dangerously hot scotch bonnet, peppers have made their way into Caribbean cooking, Indian, Korean and many other cuisines. Digestion is greatly improved as well.

Chutney: A sweet and spicy marmalade-like condiment often made from tropical fruit such as mango and pineapple, cooked along with garlic, onion, hot peppers and spices.

Cocoa: Cocoa beans are also native to South America. The Mayas transported these beans to Mexico where they became an integral part of Mexican cuisines.

Colombo: A curry introduced by Bengal immigrant workers to the French Caribbean.

Congo: An alternative name for habanero pepper or scotch bonnet, a fiery chili pepper.

Corn: Corn was considered sacred by the Aztecs, Inca and Maya being integral to their survival. Many myths, ceremonies and gods were created around the corn growth cycles.

Coo-Coo: Cornbread made with okra. Corn was an incomplete protein and native peoples often combined it with beans and fish. Occasionally corn was processed with lime or wood ash which assisted the release of niacin.

Culantro: An aromatic herb used extensively in Puerto Rico and

Trinidad.

Dhal: Split peas or lentils.

Doubles: Spicy pastry usually made from split pea flour, deep fried and may be filled with curried chick peas and vegetables.

Dasheen: Leaves of the taro plant.

Foo-Foo: Dumpling which can be made from plantain, cassava, and yam.

Guava: Ancient fruit dating back to 2500 B.C. in Peru, member of the myrtle family and related to allspice and cloves. Richly aromatic the pinky-peach fruit is used in preserves, chutneys and salads.

Jelly-nut: The soft immature meat of the coconut. Roadside vendors will hack off the top of these young coconuts and hand you a spoon. First the refreshing milky juice is consumed, then the slippery jelly spooned out.

Jerk: A marinade or rub primarily from Jamaica made from allspice, cinnamon, cloves, nutmeg and other ingredients to flavor fish, chicken and meat.

Jicama: Root vegetable with white meat recalling apples and water chestnuts.

Jug-Jug: Popular Barbados pudding made from pigeon peas.

Kucheela: Fiery condiment made from unripe mango with East Indian origins.

Mauby: Popular West Indian drink made from the bark of a carob tree.

Mango: Popular Caribbean fruit with a thin skin, deep orange color and large flat seed. Tasting like a cross between peaches, strawberries and pineapple, this fruit is used unripe and unripe extensively in Caribbean cuisine. Heavily exported.

Passionfruit: A rapidly growing vine which produces the most beautiful flowers in shades of white, red, blue and purple. The stems resemble the crucifixion. The flowers in turn become a wrinkled tart fruit with a floral fragrance used in liqueurs and drinks.

Paw paw: Papaya, native to Central America, is bright orange in color with edible black, peppery seeds. The earthy and sweet fruit is high in vitamins A and C.

Peanut: Peanuts were used by the ancient South American peoples and transported around the world to the East Indies and Africa and became the basis for sauces and stews.

Pelau: A sweet rice dish made with coconut milk, peas and meat.

Pholouri: Trinidadian fritter made from split-peas also known as Doubles.

Pigeon Peas: A legume similar to black-eyed peas known in Puerto Rico as grandules.

Pineapple: The Carib Indians used the pineapple as a symbol of hospitality and the Europeans adapted this by carving bedposts, door knockers and building corners with the pineapple. The Spanish named it pineapple because of it resemblance to a pinecone.

Plantain: Members of the banana family, this versatile fruit can be used both ripe and unripe—high in potassium.

Potato: Staple of ancient Peruvian civilization, the potato grew at high elevations were corn failed. Potatoes were introduced to Europe in the sixteenth century.

Pumpkin: This is more like a winter squash than the pumpkins we use at Halloween. *Acorn, winter or butternut squash may be substituted.*

Roti: A delicious pastry often made from garbanzo or split pea flour filled with curried vegetables, fish, chicken or meat.

Salt fish: Usually a type of cod which was heavily salted in the days before readily available refrigeration. Still very much in use today, the cod must be soaked and rinsed several times to remove the excess salt. *Grouper, scrod, halibut or any other mild flaky fish may be substituted.*

Sea moss: A sweet drink made from seaweed and cinnamon said to have aphrodisiac qualities.

Sofrito: Spanish seasoning made from onions, green peppers, chilies, garlic, culantro, oregano and ham.

Solomon Gundy: Jamaican pickled herring.

Sorrel: A type of hibiscus made into a sweet, pungent red drink.

Souse: Pickled pork parts, feet, etc.

Stamp and Go: Jamaican salt fish cakes.

Sweet Potato: Member of the morning glory family, the sweet potatoe came from Central America, rich in Vitamins A and C.

Tamarind: Originally from India, the tart brownish pulp is extracted from the pods and is used in chutneys and is a prime ingredient in Worcestershire sauce.

Tania: Root vegetable used in soups.

Taro: Starchy root vegetable.

Tomato: Tomato is another extremely old food known to man, coming from coastal Peru. Tomatoes provided a source of vitamins A and C to the basic corn diet. They were introduced to Europe in the early 1500's.

Vanilla: Native to Mexico, it is a member of the orchid family. This epiphyte, produces lovely green-yellow flowers which in turn become long green pods. The Aztecs used it to flavor their cocoa and coconut flavored drinks.

Yam: Caribbean root vegetable. *Sweet potatoe may be substituted.*

Yucca: see Cassava.

Bibliography

American Airlines. *American Eagle Lattitudes Travel Issue.* November/December 1999.

Babb, Dalton. *Cooking the West Indian Way.* Hong Kong: MacMillan Press Ltd., 1994.

Bayless, Rick, Dean Groen and Jean Marie Brownson. *Rick Bayless's Mexican Kitchen.* New York: Scribner, 1996.

Bodger, Lorraine. *Chutneys & Relishes.* New York: Simon & Schuster, 1995.

Brown, Dale M., ed. *Aztecs: Reign of Blood and Splendor.* Alexandria, VA: Time-Life Books, 1992

Brown Dale M., ed. *Indas: Lords of Gods and Glory.* Alexandria, VA: Time-Life Books, 1968.

Carias de, Maria Ramiriz. *Dominican Cookbook.* Columbia: Pilon, 1993.

Caufield, Catherine. *In the Rainforest.* Chicago: University of Chicago Press, 1984.

Chesman, Andrea. *Salsa.* Freedom, CA: The Crossing Press, 1985.

Cook's Illustrated, Bishop Jack, ed. *The Best Recipe.* Brookline, MA: Boston Common Press, 1999.

D'Amico, Sergio, Fortin Jacques. *The Visual Food Encyclopedia.* Quebec: Editions Quebec/Amerique, 1996.

DeWitt, Dave; Stock, Melissa T.; Wilan, Mary Jane. *Hot & Spicy Caribbean.* USA: Prima Publishing, 1996.

DeWitt, Dave; DeAnda, Jeanette; Mary Jane Wilan. *Meltdown The Official Fiery Foods Show Cookbook and Chilihead Resource Guide.* Freedom, CA: Crossing Press, 1995.

Fodor's. *Fodor's 2000 Caribbean.* New York: Fodor's Travel Publications, Inc., 2000.

Grigson, Jane. *Exotic Fruits and Vegetables.* New York: Henry Holt and Company, 1987.

Hafner, Dorinda. *A Taste of Africa.* Berkeley, CA: Ten Speed Press, 1993.

Hale, William Harlan. *Horizon Cookbook and Illustrated History of Eating and Drinking Through the Ages.* New York: American Heritage, 1968.

Hamilton, Edward. *Rums of the Eastern Caribbean*. Puerto Rico: Taffia Publishing, 1995.

Harris, Dunstan. *Island Barbeque*. San Francisco: Chronicle Books, 1995.

Henry, Mike. *Caribbean Cocktails & Mixed Drinks*. Jamaica: Kingston Publishers Limited, 1996.

Hyatt, Derril A. *Foods America Gave the World*. Boston: L.C. Page and Co., 1997.

Lafray, Joyce. *!Cuba Cocina!* New York: Hearst Books, 1994.

Le Blanc, Bereley. *The Complete Caribbean Cookbook*. London: Chartwell Books, 1996.

Maedac Supply Company Limited. *Some Favorites from the Cayman Islands, British West Indies*. Cayman Islands, BWI: Maedac, 1988.

Marcas, George and Nancy. *Forbidde Fruits and Forgotten Vegetables: A Guide to Cooking with Ethnic, Exotic and Neglected Produce*. New York: St. Martin's Press, 1982.

Morgan, Jefferson and Jinx. *The Sugar Mill Caribbean Cookbook*. Boston: Harvard Common Press, 1996.

Murray, Dea. *Cooking With Rum Caribbean Style*. U.S. Virgin Islands: Rolfe Associates, 1982.

Ortiz, Yvonne. *A Taste of Puerto Rico*. New York: Penguin Books, 1994.

Osborne, Laura. *The Rasta Cookbook*. Trenton, New Jersey: Africa World Press, Inc., 1988.

Padda, Dr. Darshan S. Director of the University of the Virgin Islands Cooperative Extension Service. *Native Recipes*. St. Croix, U.S. Virgin Islands: Cooperative Extension Service University of the Virgin Islands, 1994.

Pappas, Lou Seibert. *Chutneys & Relishes*. San Francisco: Chronicle Books, 1995.

Potter, Betty. *Grand Recipes from the Cayman Islands*. Cayman Islands, British West Indies: Potter Publications, 1985.

Quinn, Lucinda Scale. *Jamaican Cooking*. USA: MacMillan, 1972.

Ramirez, Julio J. and Marie Perucca. *El Cocodrilo's Cookbook*. USA: MacMillan, 1996.

Rosado, Judith & Robert. *Recipes from La Isla!* Los Angeles: Lowell House, 1995.

Seaman, George A. *Not So Cat Walk*. St. Maarten, Netherlands Antilles: Desktop Publications N.V.

Thomas, Heather. *The Essential Caribbean Cookbook*. Philadelphia: Courage Books, 1998.

Thompson, Jeanette T. *Bahamian Cuisine*. Great Exuma, Bahamas: Tract Three Productions, 1996.

Williams, Cindy. *Bahamian Cookery, Cindy's Treasures*. Nassau, Bahamas: The Nassau Guardian, 1997.

Willinsky, Helen. *Jerk Barbeque from Jamaica*. Freedom, CA: The Crossing Press, 1990.

Index